MW01116091

APPLE WATCH ULTRA 2
USER GUIDE

A Complete User Manual with Step
By Step Instruction For Beginners
And Seniors To Learn How To Use
The Apple Watch Ultra 2 Like A Pro
With WatchOS 10 Tips & Tricks

BY

HERBERT A. CLARK

Table of Contents

INTRODUCTION

Welcome to Apple Watch Ultra 2, the most powerful and capable Apple Watch ever, built for trail, track, & underwater environments. On the outside, the smartwatch features an Action button that can be used to start a workout, place, waypoints, & turn on the flashlight with just one press. The titanium coating protects the sapphire front crystal from side impact.

The Apple Watch Ultra 2 has a faster chip & a new Double-Tap feature that allows users to control the smartwatch with finger taps. The watch has a stronger case, a larger screen, and a longer battery life.

This guide will help you find all the great things the Apple Watch Ultra 2 can do.

What's in the Box

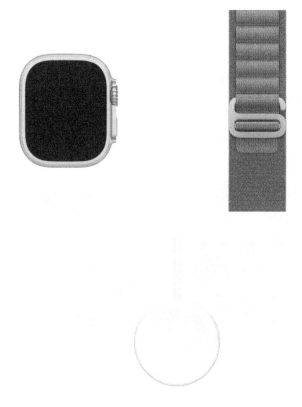

Apple Watch Magnetic Fast Charger to USB-C
Cable (1m)

FEATURES OF APPLE WATCH ULTRA 2

Design

The new Apple Watch Ultra did not receive a design update. It still has the same rounded, rectangular look like the previous generation, and it's available in 49 mm size option.

The watch measures in at 49 mm by 44 mm by 14.4 mm, and weighs 61.3g.

There's an Action button on the side of the watch that can be personalized to perform an action of your choice. The Action button can do things like open applications or start Workouts.

Materials

The new smartwatch is made of titanium, which is a light & durable material that provides corrosion resistance for use in water. The back of the watch is made of ceramic & sapphire crystal.

Durability

The Apple Watch Ultra is known for its ability to withstand very extreme temperatures. The watch functions in temperatures as warm as 131°F to as cold as -4°F.

It's certified to MIL-STD-810.0H, a standard used for military equipment. Apple says that this testing includes Vibration, Shock, Freezing Rain, Contamination by Dust, Sand, Immersion, Humidity, Rain, Fluids, etc.

Double Tap Gesture

You can now use the Double Tap gesture to control your watch. When you double-tap your thumb & index finger, your smartwatch's sensor detects the movement and activates what is on your screen, allowing you to do things like start or stop a timer, pause or play songs, end calls, answer calls, and more.

Storage

The new watch has 64 GB of storage space

Health Features

The Apple Watch Ultra 2 offers health monitoring features like an optical heart-rate sensor that calculates metrics such as high heart-rate, resting heart-rate, & calories burned. You can also use the electric heart rate sensor to take an ECG, while the infrared light & LEDs allow users to track blood oxygen level. An inbuilt gyroscope & accelerometer allows other important health-related features like Fall Detection to work properly.

The Apple Watch Ultra can detect irregular, high & low heart rates. It can also detect health issues like AFib & send you an alert when it detects anomalies.

Battery life

The Apple Watch Ultra has a 564mAh battery that can last for about 36 hours, which can be increased to about 72 hours with the Low Power Mode.

Siren

The new smartwatch has an 86-decibel emergency siren that can be used to call attention to a location in an emergency. The sound makes use of 2 alternating patterns, including a distress pattern and another that matches the standard SOS pattern.

Apple claims that the siren can be heard from about 600ft away. You can activate the Siren by long-pressing the Side button or the Action button.

APPLE WATCH ULTRA 2

Digital Crown

Side button

Action button

Mic

Speaker

Action button

Speaker/Siren

Depth gauge/
Water Temp sensor

Digital Crown

Mic

Side button

Mic

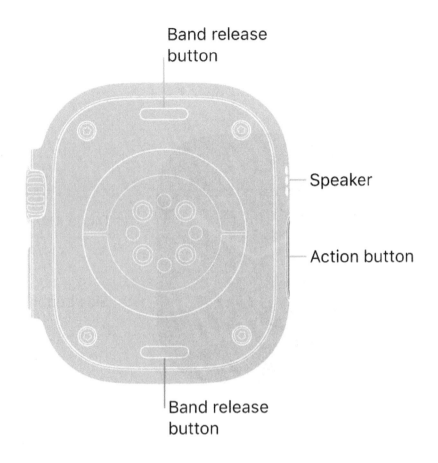

Band release
button

Speaker

Action button

Band release
button

SET UP APPLE WATCH ULTRA 2

Getting Started

❖ Ensure your iPhone has been updated to the latest iOS version. Enter the Settings application on your phone, touch the **General** button, and then touch Software Updates.
❖ Ensure your iPhone has Bluetooth activated and is connected to a mobile or WiFi network. To check, simply swipe down from the upper right edge of your phone display to reveal the Controls Centre. Bluetooth & WiFi (or mobile) buttons must be enabled.

Step 1: Switch on and pair your smartwatch

❖ Wear your smartwatch and make sure it's not too tight or loose on your wrist.
❖ To switch on your smartwatch, simply long-press the side button till the Apple symbol appears on the screen.

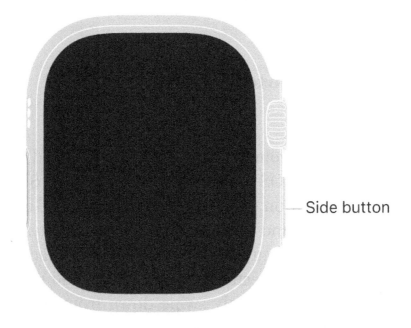

Side button

❖ Hold your smartwatch close to your phone, wait for the pairing screen to appear on your phone, and then click on the **Continue** button.

Or, enter the Apple Watch application on your phone, and touch the **Pair New Watch** button.

❖ Click on the **Setup for Myself** option.
❖ Set your phone in a way that the watch face can be seen in the view finder. Wait to see an alert stating that your smartwatch has been connected to your phone.

If you cannot make use of the camera, or the animation doesn't appear, or your phone cannot read it, click on **Pair Manually**, and then follow the instructions

Step 2: Setup your watch

❖ If this is your 1st Apple Watch Ultra, click on the **Setup Apple Watch** button, and then adhere to the directives on your phone & watch to complete setup.
If you have paired another Apple smartwatch with your iPhone before, you will see a screen that says "**Make This Your New Watch**". Touch App & Data and Settings to see how Express Set up is going to configure your new smartwatch. Then touch the **Continue** button. Touch the **Customize Setting** option if you want to choose how your new smartwatch will be configured. Then select one of the backups from your previous Apple Watch to restore. Or, if you want to fully personalize your watch's settings, click on the **Setup as New Apple Watch** option.

❖ Adhere to the directives on your display to setup the following:
  ➤ Insert your Apple ID details.
  ➤ Create a passcode for your smartwatch.

> ➤ Adjust the size of the text, enter your personal info like your birthdate and height

for fitness and health purposes, and select the health alerts you would like to receive.

You can change these settings after setting up your watch.

Step: 3 Setup cellular & Apple Pay

You can activate mobile service on your smartwatch during setup, or you can do it later in the Watch application on your iPhone.

Next, you will be prompted to setup Apple Pay by adding cards. Then your smartphone will walk you through features like the Always On Display.

Allow your devices to synchronize

Your smartwatch will display the watch face when the pairing process has been completed. Keep your phone near your watch so that both devices can continue to synchronize data in the background

Unpair your smartwatch

❖ Enter the Watch application on your phone.
❖ Touch the **My Watch** tab, and then click on
the **All Watches** button.

❖ Click on the Info button ⓘ beside the Apple Watch, and then click on the **Unpair Apple Watch** button.

Pair more than one watch

You can connect another Apple smartwatch the same way you connected the first one. Or adhere to the guidelines below:

❖ Head over to the Watch application on your smartphone.
❖ Touch the **My Watch** tab, and then touch the **All Watches** button.
❖ Touch the **Add Watch** option, and then adhere to the directives on the screen.

Quickly switch to another Apple smartwatch

Your smartphone will detect the paired Apple Watch you are putting on & automatically connect to it. Simply wear another Apple Watch & lift your hand.

You can also select an Apple smartwatch manually:

❖ Navigate to the Watch application on your phone.
❖ Touch the **My Watch** tab, and then click on the **All Watches** button.
❖ Disable the **Auto-Switch** feature, and then pick another watch.

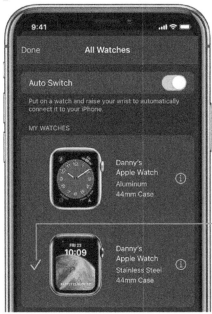

The active Apple Watch.

To know if your smartwatch is connected to your phone, long-press your watch's side button to show the Controls Center, and then look for the Connection Status logo

BASIC SETTINGS

Basic gestures

You can use the following gestures to interact with your smartwatch.

❖ Touch: Gently use your finger to tap the screen.

❖ Swipe: Move one of your fingers across the display—right, left, down, or up.

❖ Drag: Swipe across the screen without raising your finger.

Choose a function for the Action button

During setup, you are asked to select a function for the Action button. The Options include:

Action button

Action	Press
Waypoint	Press the button to Drop a Compass Waypoint
Stopwatch	1st press: Start 2nd press: Mark lap

Workout	1st press: Launch the Workout application or begin a workout session. 2nd press: Depends on the workout selected
Dive	Press: Begin a dive
Backtrack	Press to record the path
Flashlight	1st press: Turn on the flashlight 2nd press: Turn off the flashlight

Shortcut	**Press to begin a shortcut**

Some applications offer more options when you press the Side button & the Action button at the same time. For instance, if you configure the Action button to begin a stopwatch, press the Side & Action buttons at the same time to pause the stopwatch.

To change the function of the Action button, simply enter the Settings application on your smartwatch, touch **Action Button**, and then touch **Action** to select one of the options.

The Apple Watch application

In the Watch application on your iPhone, you can change your watch settings, personalize watch faces, install applications, etc.

❖ Touch the Apple Watch application icon on your iPhone's Home Screen or Apps Library.

❖ Touch the **My Watch** tab to view your watch settings

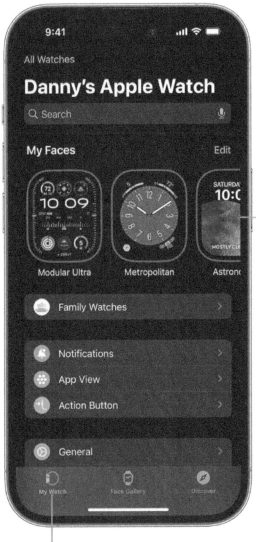

Swipe to see your watch face collection.

Settings for Apple Watch.

Charge your smartwatch

Setup the charger

❖ Put the charging cable or charger on a flat surface in a well-ventilated space.

The Apple Watch Ultra comes with a Magnetic Fast Charger to USB-C cable.

❖ Connect the charging cable to the power adapter.
❖ Connect the power adapter to the power outlet.

Start charging

Place the Magnetic charger or charging cable on the back of your watch. The concave end of the charger will snap to the back of your watch & align neatly.

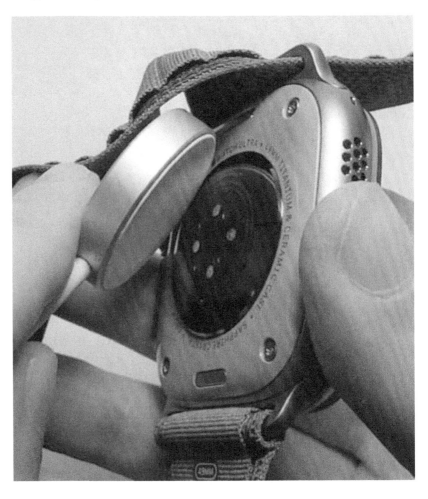

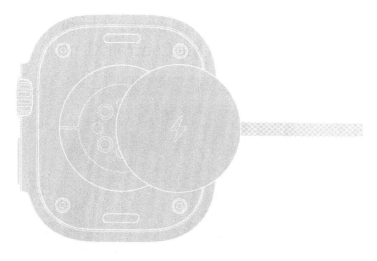

Your watch will play a chime when it starts charging (unless it's in silent mode) & show a charge logo ⚡ on the watch face. The logo turns red when your watch's battery is low, and changes to green when it's connected to power.

You can also charge your smartwatch in a flat position or on its side.

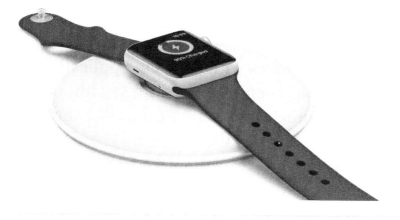

To check the remaining power, simply press the side button to reveal the Controls Centre.

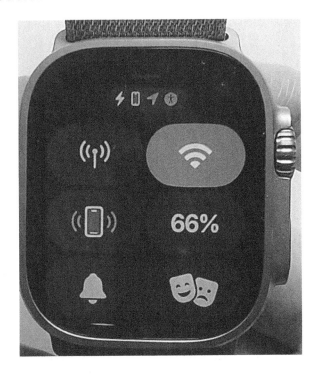

Open applications on your smartwatch

Your watch comes with different applications that can help you keep track of your health, exercise, etc. To launch an application, just press the Digital Crown, and then click on the app's icon. Press the Digital Crown one more time to return to your Watch's Home Screen.

From the watch face, press to see the Home Screen.

Tap to open an app.

Wake your watch display

You can wake your smartwatch display in the following ways:

❖ Raise your hand. Your watch will go back to sleep when you put your wrist down.
❖ Tap the screen
❖ Press the Digital Crown or rotate it upward.

If you do not want your smartwatch to wake when you rotate the Digital Crown upward or raise your hand, simply navigate to the Settings app on your smartwatch, touch Display & Brightness, then deactivate Wake on Crown Rotation & Wake on Wrist Raise.

Low Power mode

Activate the Low Power mode to save battery life. Doing so turns off heart rate notifications, background blood oxygen & heart rate measurements, and Always On display. Cellular is deactivated till when it's needed—for instance, when you send a message.

Note: The low power mode will automatically turn off when the battery is 80 percent charged.

- ❖ Press your watch's side button to enter the Controls Centre.
- ❖ Touch the battery percentage, and then activate Low Power Mode.
- ❖ Scroll down and click on **Turn On** to confirm your selection.
  You can click on the **Turn On For** button, and then select one of the options.

To switch back to normal power mode, simply press your watch's side button to enter the Controls Centre, touch the battery percentage, and then deactivate Low Power Mode.

See the time since the last charge

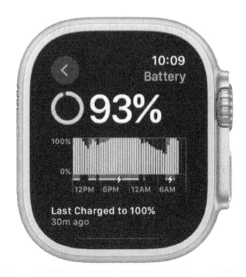

❖ Enter the Settings application
❖ Touch the **Battery** button
The battery screen will show the remaining battery percentage, recent battery charge history, and the last time your smartwatch was charged.

Check battery health

Check your watch's battery capacity relative to when it was new.

❖ Navigate to the Settings application.
❖ Touch the **Battery** button, and then touch Battery Health.
Your smartwatch will alert you if the battery capacity is significantly reduced

Optimize battery charging

To reduce the aging of the battery, your smartwatch makes use of machine learning to learn your charging patterns, with this information it'll make sure the battery doesn't charge above 80% till you need to use it.

- ❖ Navigate to the Settings application.
- ❖ Click on the **Battery** button, and then click on **Battery Health**.
- ❖ Activate Optimized Charge Limit

Stop applications from refreshing in the background

When you switch to another application, the application you were using may still check for new contents & updates in the background.

Refreshing applications in the background can use power. You can deactivate this feature to increase your watch's battery life.

- ❖ Navigate to the Settings application.
- ❖ Head over to General, then click on Background Apps Refresh
- ❖ Disable the **Background Apps Refresh** feature to stop all applications from refreshing. Or scroll, and deactivate the feature for each app.

Use double tap to perform common actions on your smartwatch

On your smartwatch, tap your thumb & index finger together two times to reply to a message, answer a call, etc. When you use the **double tap** gesture, the Double Tap icon will appear in the upper part of your screen. If you use the double-tap gesture and it isn't available on a specific screen, the Double Tap icon will shake from side to side.

Adhere to the directives below to choose what a double tap gesture does when browsing your smart stack or playing media.

- ❖ Enter the Settings application.
- ❖ Touch the **Gestures** button, click on the **Double Tap** button, and then select from the following options:
  - ➢ Smart Stack: Pick Select or Advance
  - ➢ Playback: Select Skip or Pause/Play
- ❖ Deactivate the **Double Tap** feature if you do not want to use the feature on your device.

Turn your smartwatch on & off

❖ Switch on: Long-press the side button till you see the Apple logo on your screen.

❖ Turn off: Long-press the side button till the slider appears on your screen, touch the Power Off button  in the upper right, and then drag the Power Off slider to the right end.

When your smartwatch is switched off, you can long-press the Digital Crown to make your watch show the time.

Note: You cannot switch off your device while it is charging. First, unplug it from its charger and then switch it off.

Always On

The Always On feature allows your smartwatch to show the watch face & time even when you put your hand down. When you lift your wrist, your smartwatch will function fully.

❖ Enter the Settings application.
❖ Touch Display & Brightness, and then touch the **Always On** button
❖ Enable the Always On feature, and then touch the options below to set them up

- ➢ Show Apps: Select the applications that should appear when you put your wrist down
- ➢ Show Complications Data: Select the complications that will display data when you put your hand down
- ➢ Show Notifications: Select the notifications that should appear when you put your hand down

Go back to clock face

You can select how long your smartwatch stays before going back to the clock face from an open application.

- ❖ Navigate to the Settings application.
- ❖ Touch General> Returns to Clock, and then select any of the options
- ❖ You can also press the Digital Crown to go to the clock face from any application

Wake to last activity

For many applications, you can set your smartwatch to go back to where you were before it went to sleep.

- ❖ Navigate to the Settings application.
- ❖ Touch General> Returns to Clock, scroll down and click on one of the applications, then enable the **Return to App** feature

Or, launch the Watch application on your iPhone, touch the **My Watch** tab, and then head over to General> Return to Clock.

Keep your smartwatch display on longer

- ❖ Navigate to the Settings application.
- ❖ Click on Display & Brightness, touch Wake Duration, and then select an option.

Lock or unlock your watch

Unlock your smartwatch

You can insert your passcode to unlock your smartwatch manually or set it to automatically unlock when you unlock your paired iPhone.

* Enter your watch's passcode: Wake your smartwatch, and then insert your watch's passcode.
* Unlock your smartwatch when you unlock your phone: Enter the Watch application on your phone, touch the **My Watch** button, touch the **Passcode** button, and then enable the **Unlock with iPhone** feature.
  Your phone has to be within the standard Bluetooth range (approximately 33ft) of your smartwatch to unlock it.

Change your passcode

* Enter the Settings application.
* Touch the **Passcode** button, touch Change Passcode, and then adhere to the directives on your display.

Or, launch the Watch application on your phone, click on the **My Watch** button, touch Passcode, then touch Change Passcode and adhere to the directives on your display.

Tip: To use a longer passcode, enter the Settings application on your smartwatch, touch the **Passcode** button, and then deactivate Simple Passcode.

Turn off the passcode

❖ Navigate to the Settings application.
❖ Click on the **Passcode** button, and then click on Turn Off Passcode.

Or, launch the Watch application on your phone, click on the **My Watch** button, touch Passcode, and then touch Turn Off Passcode.

Auto lock

By default, your smartwatch automatically locks when you aren't putting it on. Adhere to the directives below to change the wrist detection setting.

❖ Navigate to the Settings application on your smartwatch.
❖ Click on Passcode, and then enable or disable **Wrist Detection**.

Deactivating Wrist Detection will affect these features:

- When making use of Apple Pay on your device, you will be asked to insert your password when you want to authenticate payment.
- Heart rate monitoring & notifications are deactivated.
- Some Activity metrics are not available.
- Your smartwatch will not automatically make an emergency call even after detecting a hard-impact fall.
- Your smartwatch will no longer automatically lock & unlock.

Lock your watch manually

Before you can manually lock your smartwatch, you have to first deactivate Wrist Detection. (Enter the Settings application, touch Passcode, and then deactivate Wrist Detection)

❖ Press your watch's side button to reveal the Controls Centre
❖ Click on the Lock button

You'll need to insert your passcode when next you try to use your watch.

If you forgot your passcode

If you forgot your passcode simply unpair your smartwatch from your phone to erase its settings & password, and then pair it again.

Erase your data after ten consecutive wrong passcode entries

To protect your data if your device is stolen or lost, simply set it to delete all data after ten consecutive wrong passcode entries.

* Navigate to the Settings application.
* Click on Passcode, and then enable **Erase Data**.

Select a language or region

* Launch the Watch application on your phone.
* Touch the **My Watch** button, head over to General> Language and Region, touch Custom, and then select one of the languages.

To add a language, click on the **Add Language** button, and then select from the available options.

Switch Digital Crown or wrist orientation

If you want to move your smartwatch to your other hand, simply change the orientation settings so that lifting your hand wakes your smartwatch, and rotating the Digital Crown moves things the way you expect.

❖ Navigate to the Settings application
❖ Head over to General> Orientation

You can also launch the Watch application on your phone, click on the **My Watch** button, and then head over to General>Watch Orientation

Wear your Apple Watch

The back of your watch has to touch your skin for features like electrical & optical heart sensors, Taptic Engine, and Wrist Detection to function properly. Wearing your smartwatch in the right way— not too loose, not too tight, and with space for your skin to breathe—keeps you comfortable and allows the sensors to work well.

You may want to tighten your smartwatch band when working out, and loosen it a bit when you are done. In addition, the sensors only work when you're wearing the watch on the top of your wrist.

Too loose

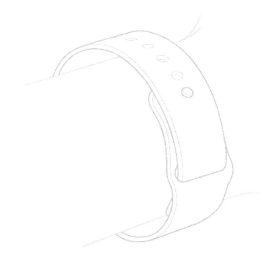

If your smartwatch does not stay in place, or the sensor cannot read your heartrate, tighten the band a little.

Perfect

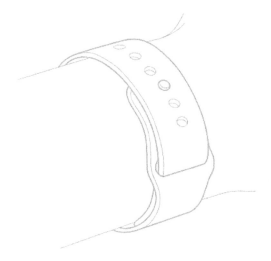

The smartwatch should be snug but comfortable.

Remove, replace, & adjust your watch bands

Ensure you're using a band that corresponds to the size of your smartwatch.

Remove & change a band

❖ Press & hold the band release button on your smartwatch.
❖ Slide the band to remove it from your watch, and then slide another band in.

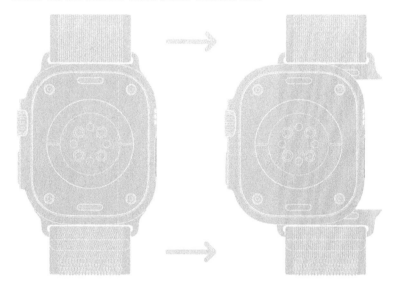

Don't ever force a watch band into the slot. If you are having difficulty inserting or removing a band, simply press & hold the band release button again.

Tighten the band

For best performance, your smartwatch needs to fit closely on your hand.

Tip: When using an Ocean band, move the loop very close to the buckle for a more secure fit during high-impact water sports.

Tip: When using a Trail Loop band, attach the folded side of the band to the top of your smartwatch for a more secure fit during high-impact water sports.

Check for & install software updates

❖ Launch the Watch application on your phone.
❖ Click on the **My Watch** button, head over to General> Software Updates, and if there's an update, click Download and Install.

Or, enter the Settings application on your smartwatch, and then head over to General> Software Updates.

CUSTOMIZE YOUR WATCH

Open applications on your smartwatch

Your watch comes with different applications that can help you keep track of your health, exercise, etc.

From the watch face, press to see the Home Screen.

Tap to open an app.

Display your applications in list or grid view

The Home Screen can show applications in the list or grid view. Adhere to the directives below to choose one of the views:

- ❖ From the watch face, press the Digital Crown to display your watch's Home Screen.
- ❖ Rotate the Digital Crown to scroll down, and then select List View or Grid View.

Or, enter the Settings application, touch App View, and then select one of the options.

Open applications from the Home Screen

How you launch applications depends on the view you're using.

- ❖ Grid View: Touch an application icon. Rotate the Digital Crown to view more applications.

❖ List view: Rotate the Digital Crown, and then touch one of the applications.

Press the Digital Crown to go back to the Home Screen from an application, and press it one more time to go to the watch face.

Use the Action button

You can use the Action button to initiate a range of functions. For instance, press the Action button to open applications & trigger features suited to a favourite activity.

- ❖ Enter the Settings application.
- ❖ Click on Action Button, and then click on Action to select one of the actions, like Dive, Backtrack, or Workout.
- ❖ Touch the Back icon , and then select other options, if available.

  For instance, if you select Workout, click on the Back icon to go back to the actions list, and then touch First Press to select a workout to launch when you press the Action button.

Some applications offer more options when you press the Side button & the Action button simultaneously. For instance, if you configure the Action button to begin a stopwatch, press the Side button & Action button simultaneously to pause the stopwatch.

Open an application from the Apps Switcher

- ❖ Press the Digital Crown twice quickly, and then rotate the Digital Crown to scroll through your recently used applications.
- ❖ Touch one of the applications to open it.

Turn the Digital Crown to see more apps. Tap one to open it.

Remove an application from the Apps Switcher

Press the Digital Crown twice quickly, and then rotate the Digital Crown to go to the application you would like to remove. Swipe the application to the left, and then touch **X**.

Swipe left on an app, then tap the X.

Organize applications on your smartwatch

Reorder your applications in grid view

❖ Press the Digital Crown to enter the Home Screen.
  If you're using the list view, enter the Settings application, touch App View, and then touch Grid View.
❖ Long-press an application and then drag the application to another location on your screen.
❖ Press the Digital Crown when you are done.

Touch and hold an app, then drag to a new location.

Or, enter the Watch application on your phone, click on the **My Watch** button, touch Apps View, and then touch the **Arrangement** button. Long-press an application icon, and then drag the application to another location on the screen.

Note: In the list view, applications are always arranged alphabetically.

Touch and hold an app, then drag to a new location.

Remove an application from your smartwatch

Long-press the Home screen and then touch the **X** button to delete the application from your smartwatch. It'll remain on your paired phone unless you remove it from there as well.

In list view, swipe an application to the left, and then touch the Trash icon to delete it from your smartwatch.

If you delete an application from your phone, that application will also be deleted from your smartwatch.

Adjust application settings

❖ Enter the Watch application on your phone.
❖ Click on the **My Watch** button, and then scroll down to view the applications you've installed.
❖ Touch one of the applications to adjust its settings.

View the storage used by applications

You can see how the storage on your smartwatch is being used—the total storage used, how much is left, and how much storage each application is using.

❖ Enter the Settings application
❖ Head over to General> Storage

Or, enter the Watch application on your phone, click on the **My Watch** button, and then head over to General > Storage.

Get more applications on your smartwatch

You can install applications from the App Store on your smartwatch or install applications you already have on your iPhone.

Note: To automatically download the companion iOS version of an application you have added to your smartwatch, navigate to the Settings application on your watch, click on Apps Store, and then enable Automatic Downloads. Ensure you also have **Automatic Updates** activated to get the latest version of your Watch applications.

Install applications from the Apps Store

* ❖ Launch the Apps Store application on your smartwatch.
* ❖ Rotate the Digital Crown to view collections & applications.
* ❖ Touch one of the collections to view more applications
* ❖ Touch the **Get** button to get a free application. Touch the price to buy the application.

    If there's a Re-download icon ☁ instead of a price, it means you have already bought the application and can download it again for free.

To look for a specific application, click on the Search icon 🔍 in the upper part of your display, then type, or use the Scribble or Dictation feature to type the name of the application. You can also click on a category to view subcategories of applications.

To use the Scribble feature, swipe up from the lower edge of your screen, and then click on the **Scribble** button.

Install applications you already have on your phone

By default, applications on your phone that have a WatchOS application available are installed automatically and appear on your watch's Home Screen. To instead choose to install certain applications, simply adhere to the directives below:

❖ Navigate to the Watch application on your phone.
❖ Click on the **My Watch** button, touch the **General** button, and then disable Automatic Apps Install.

- ❖ Click on the **My Watch** button, and then scroll to **Available Apps**
- ❖ Touch the **Install** button beside the applications you would like to install.

Tell the time on your smartwatch

There are many ways to tell the time on your smartwatch.

- ❖ Raise your hand: The time will appear on the watch face and in the upper-right corner of many applications.
- ❖ Hear the time: Navigate the Setting application on your smartwatch, click on Clock, and then enable the **Speak Time** feature. Hold 2 of your fingers on the watch face to hear the time. You can set your watch to play chimes on the hour. To do this, just navigate the Setting application on your smartwatch, click on Clock, and then enable **Chimes**. Click on Sounds to select one of the options.
- ❖ Feel the time: To feel the time tapped on your wrist when you activate silent mode on your watch, simply navigate the Settings application, click on the **Clock** button, click on **Taptic Time**,

enable Taptic Time, and then pick one of the options.

>Note: If Taptic-Time is deactivated, your watch might be set to always say the time. Before you can use Taptic Time, first navigate to the Settings app, click on the Clock button, and then enable **Controls with Silent Mode** below Speak Time.

❖ Use Siri: Raise your hand & say "What's the time?"

Control Center

The Control Center provides an easy way to activate theater mode, turn on the flashlight, put your watch in silent mode, etc.

Open or close the Controls Centre

❖ Press your watch's side button to open the Controls Centre.
❖ Close the Controls Centre: While in the Controls Centre, press your watch's side button to close the Controls Centre.

Check the Controls Centre status

The Small icons in the upper part of the Controls Centre show the status of some settings— such as whether your smartwatch is connected to a mobile network, & whether features like DND or Airplane Mode are active.

Open the Controls Center to see the status icons. Touch the icons to view details.

Rearrange Controls Center

Follow the steps below to rearrange the Controls Centre:

- ❖ Press your watch's side button to reveal the Controls Center.
- ❖ Scroll down to the end of the Controls Center, and then click on the **Edit** button.
- ❖ Long-press one of the buttons, and then drag it to another location
- ❖ Touch the **Done** button when you are done.

Remove Controls Centre buttons

Follow the directives below to remove the buttons in Control Centre:

- ❖ Press your watch's side button to reveal the Controls Center.
- ❖ Scroll down to the end of the Controls Center, and then click on the **Edit** button.
- ❖ Click on the Remove icon ⊖ in the corner of the button you would like to erase.
- ❖ Touch the **Done** button when you are done.

To restore a deleted button, open the Controls Centre, click on the **Edit** button, and click the Add icon ⊕ in the corner of the button you would like to restore. Touch the **Done** button when you are done.

Enable airplane mode

Some airlines will allow you to travel with your watch switched on if it is in airplane mode. By default, enabling Airplane mode deactivates WiFi & mobile network and keeps Bluetooth activated. However, you can change what settings are enabled & disabled when you activate airplane mode.

❖ Enable Airplane Mode: Press your watch's side button to enter the Controls Centre, and then click on the **Airplane Mode** button.

Turn Airplane Mode on or off.

❖ Put your smartwatch & phone in Airplane mode in one step: Enter the Watch application on your phone, click on the **My Watch** button, head over to General> Airplane mode, and then enable the **Mirror iPhone** feature. When your smartwatch & iPhone are within standard Bluetooth range (about 10m), any time you activate Airplane Mode on one device, the other activates to match.

❖ Change which settings are enabled or disabled in Airplane Mode: Navigate to the Settings application on your smartwatch, touch Airplane Mode, and then select whether to enable or disable Bluetooth or WiFi by default when you activate Airplane Mode.

To enable or disable Bluetooth or WiFi while your watch is in Airplane mode, simply enter the Settings application, and then touch Bluetooth or WiFi.

When Airplane Mode is active, the Airplane Mode icon will appear in the upper part of your display.

Note: Even when Mirror iPhone is enabled, you must deactivate Airplane Mode separately on your phone & smartwatch.

Use flashlight on your smartwatch

Use your watch's flashlight to illuminate objects near you.

❖ Turn on the flashlight: Press your watch's side button to enter the Controls Center, and then click on the Flashlight button 🔦 . Swipe left to select one of the modes.

❖ Rotate the Digital Crown to change the brightness level.

❖ Press the side button or Digital Crown to switch off the flashlight.

Use Theater Mode

Turn theater mode on or off.

Theater mode stops your watch's screen from turning on when you lift your hand. It also activates silent mode.

Press your watch's side button to reveal the Controls Centre, click on the Theater button 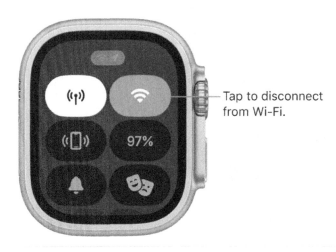, and then click on **Theater Mode.**

When theater mode is active, the theater mode icon will appear in the upper part of your display.

To wake your smartwatch when theater mode is active, touch the screen, and press the side button or Digital Crown.

Activate or deactivate WiFi

Tap to disconnect from Wi-Fi.

Press your watch's side button to enter the Controls Centre, and then click on the WiFi button  to activate or deactivate WiFi.

Tip: Long-press the WiFi button in the Controls Centre to quickly open WiFi settings on your smartwatch.

Enable or disable silent mode

Press your watch's side button to enter the Controls Centre, and then click on the Silent Mode button to activate or deactivate silent mode.

Or, enter the Watch application on your phone, touch the **My Watch** button, touch Sound & Haptics, and then activate Silent mode.

Tip: When your smartwatch receives a notification, rest your palm on your watch screen for about 3 seconds to mute it. Ensure you activate the **Cover to Mute** feature on your smartwatch—enter the Settings application, touch Sound and Haptics, and then enable the **Cover to Mute** feature.

Ping & locate your iPhone

The Precision Finding feature allows your smartwatch to ping your nearby iPhone 15 & receive directions to the phone.

❖ Press your watch's side button to reveal the Controls Centre, and then touch the Ping iPhone button ⁽ᵢ⁾.
Your phone will play a sound & if your smartwatch is in range, the screen will show a general distance & heading to your phone—for instance, 65 ft.

❖ Click on the Ping iPhone button  on your watch screen to play a sound on your phone as you locate it.

❖ Follow the heading displayed on your watch's screen, and adjust as the heading moves.
When you get close to your phone, your watch display will turn to green and your phone will Ping twice.

Tip: If you are in a dark place, long-press the Ping button to make your iPhone flash.

Find your watch

iOS 17 allows iPhone users to find their Apple Watch if it is close to them.

❖ Navigate to the Settings application on your iPhone
❖ Click on the **Control Centre** button, scroll down, and then click on the Add icon beside **Ping My Watch.**

❖ When you want to find your smartwatch, simply open the Control Centre on your iPhone and then touch the **Ping** button

Focus

The Focus feature can help you to focus when you want to concentrate on a task. The Focus feature can lessen distractions & let other applications & individuals know that you are busy.

You can select from the available Focus modes or create one.

Note: If you would like to share your Focus settings with all the Apple devices signed in with your Apple ID, enter the Settings application on your phone, touch **Focus**, and then activate **Share Across Devices**.

Activate or deactivate Focus

❖ Press your watch's side button to reveal the Controls Center.
❖ Press & hold the current **Focus** button.

If no focus mode is active, the Controls Centre will display the DND icon  .

❖ Touch a Focus mode

❖ Choose any of the Focus options—On for an hour, On, etc.

To deactivate a Focus mode, simply click on the Focus button in the Controls Center.

When a Focus mode is turned on, you'll see its icon in the upper part of the watch face, in the Controls Center, & beside the time in applications.

Create your own focus

❖ Navigate to the Settings application on your smartphone, and then click on the **Focus** button.

❖ Click on the Add icon +, choose one of the Focus, and then adhere to the directives on the screen.

Select a focus watch face

You can set a watch face to appear when a specific Focus mode is turned on. For instance, when you turn on the Work Focus mode, your smartwatch can show a Simple watch face.

❖ Navigate to the Settings application on your smartphone, and then click on the **Focus** button.
❖ Click on one of the Focus modes, and then click on Choose under the Watch image.
❖ Choose any of the watch faces, and then click on **Done**

Create a Focus schedule

You can schedule when a Focus mode automatically activates on your watch. For instance, you can set the Work Focus mode to automatically activate at 9:31AM & deactivate at 12:31PM, from Monday to Friday. From 12:31PM to 1:31PM you may have no Focus. Then, begin the Work Focus mode again from 1:31PM to 4:31PM, Monday-Thursday.

❖ Navigate to the Settings application on your watch.

- ❖ Touch **Focus**, and then click on one of the Focus modes
- ❖ Click on **Add New**.
- ❖ Touch the From & To options and insert when you want the Focus mode to automatically start & stop.
- ❖ Scroll down the list, and select the days you want the Focus to be active.
- ❖ Touch the Back icon< in the upper left edge of your display to save the Focus.
- ❖ Repeat the steps above to add more events to the Focus mode.

Delete or turn off a Focus schedule

- ❖ Deactivate a Focus schedule: Enter the Settings application, click on Focus, and then touch one of the Focus modes. Click on a schedule, scroll, and then disable **Enabled**. Activate **Enabled** when you want to turn on the schedule again.

❖ Erase a Focus schedule: Enter the Settings application on your smartwatch, click on the **Focus** button, and then click on one of the Focus modes. Touch one of the schedules, scroll down, and then click on the **Delete** button.

Adjust brightness level & text size

Navigate to the Settings application, and touch Display and Brightness to change the below:

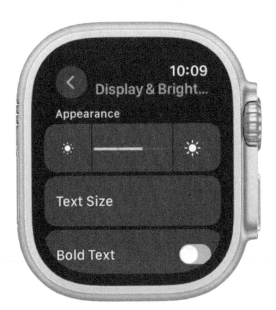

- ❖ Brightness: Click on the Brightness control to change the brightness level.
- ❖ Text size: Touch the **Text Size** button, and then rotate the Digital Crown.
- ❖ Bold Text: Activate Bold Text.

Change sound level

- ❖ Navigate to the Settings application
- ❖ Click on Sounds and Haptics
- ❖ Touch the volume controls in the Alert Volume section or touch the slider, and then rotate the Digital Crown to change the volume level.

Or, enter the Watch application on your phone, touch the **Sound and Haptics** button, and then slide the Alert Volume slider.

Adjust the haptic strength

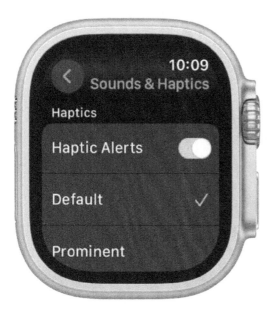

You can change the intensity of the haptics or wrist taps your smartwatch uses for alerts.

- ❖ Navigate to the Settings application.
- ❖ Click on the **Sound & Haptics** button, and then activate Haptic Alert
- ❖ Select Prominent or Default

You can also enter the Watch application on your phone, touch the **My Watch** button, touch **Sound and Haptics**, and then select one of the options.

Enable or disable Digital Crown haptics

On your smartwatch, you feel clicks when you rotate the Digital Crown to scroll. Adhere to the directives below to activate or deactivate these haptics:

❖ Navigate to the Settings application
❖ Click on **Sound & Haptics**, and then activate or deactivate Crown Haptics.
  You can also activate or deactivate system haptics.

You can also enter the Watch application, click on the **My Watch** tab, touch Sound & Haptics, and then activate or deactivate Crown Haptics.

Use Taptic Time

Your smartwatch can tap out the time on your wrist when it's in silent mode.

❖ Navigate to the Settings application.
❖ Touch the **Clock** button, scroll down, and then click on **Taptic Time**.
❖ Activate Taptic Time, and then select one of the settings —Morse Code, Terse, & Digits.
  ➢ Digits: Your smartwatch will long tap your wrist for every ten hours, short tap for every hour that follows, long tap for every ten minutes, and then short tap for every minute that follows.
  ➢ Terse: Your smartwatch will long tap your wrist for every 5 hours, short tap your wrist for the remaining hours, and then long tap you for each quarter hour.
  ➢ Morse code: Your smartwatch will tap each digit of the time on your wrist in Morse code.

Or, enter the Watch application on your phone, touch the **My Watch** button, head over to Clock> Taptics Time, and then activate it.

See & respond to notifications on your smartwatch

Apps can send notifications to keep you informed. Your smartwatch can show the notifications as they come in, but if you do not read them right away, you can check them later.

Respond to messages when they arrive

❖ If you feel or hear a notification, simply lift your hand to check it out.
How notifications appear depend on whether the screen is active or inactive.

> Active screen: A small banner will appear in the upper part of your screen.
> Inactive Screen: A full-screen notification will appear.

❖ Touch the alert to go through it.
❖ To clear a notification, simply scroll to the end of the notification, and then touch the **Dismiss** button.

View notifications you have not responded to

Notifications that you do not respond to when they arrive are automatically stored in the Notifications Centre. A red dot in the upper part of your watch face indicates that you have unread notifications.

Swipe down to view unread notifications.

Adhere to the directives below to view the notifications:

* ❖ From the watch face, swipe down to enter the Notifications Centre. From any other screen, long-press the upper part of your display, and then swipe down.
  Note: You cannot open the Notifications Centre from your watch's Home Screen. Instead, go back to the watch face or enter an application, and then open the Notifications Centre.
* ❖ Swipe down or up or rotate the Digital Crown to scroll
* ❖ Touch one of the notifications to go through it or respond to it

Tip: You can tell Siri to read a notification in the Notifications Centre to you. Simply say "Read my notifications".

To delete a message from the Notification Center without reading it, simply swipe left on the notification and then touch the **X** button. To delete all the notifications, scroll to the top of your display, and then click on the **Clear All** button.

Tip: To prevent the red dot from appearing on the watch face, navigate to the Settings application, click on **Notifications**, and then deactivate Notification Indicator.

Silence all notifications

Press your watch's side key to enter the Controls Centre, and then touch the Silent Mode button .

You'll still feel a tap when your watch receives a notification. Follow the steps below to prevent taps & sound:

❖ Press your watch's side key to enter the Controls Centre, and then touch the DND button or the active Focus mode.

❖ Click on the DND button, and then select one of the options.

Tip: When your smartwatch receives a notification, rest your palm on your watch screen for about 3 seconds to mute it. Ensure you activate the **Cover to Mute** feature on your smartwatch—enter the Settings application, touch Sound and Haptics, and then enable the **Cover to Mute** feature.

Use Smart Stack to display widgets on your smartwatch

Smart Stack is a group of widgets that makes use of info like the time, place, and your task to automatically show widgets that are relevant for that time of your day. For instance, in the morning, the Weather will display the forecast, or when traveling, Smart Stack will display the boarding pass from your wallet.

Open the Smart Stack

❖ Press the Digital Crown to go to the watch face.
❖ Rotate the Digital Crown to scroll down till you reach the widgets section.
❖ Keep scrolling till you reach the widget you want to use, and then touch the widget to open its associated application

Tip: At the end of the Smart Stack, you'll see a widget with 3 featured applications—Messages, Workouts, & Music. Touch one of the applications to launch it.

Add & remove widgets

The Smart Stack consists of a set of preconfigured widgets that can be added, & removed. Simply scroll down from the watch face, long-press the Smart Stack, and then carry out any of the below:

❖ Add widgets: Touch the Add icon +, then touch one of the featured widgets or touch an application that appears under All Apps.
❖ Remove Widgets: Click the Remove button ⊖ .

Touch the **Done** button when you are done.

Manage your Apple ID settings

You can view & change your Apple ID information.

Change your personal info

❖ Navigate to the Settings application.
❖ Click on [Your Name], click on the **Personal Information** button, and then carry out any of the below:
  ➢ Change your name: Click on your name, and then click on the Last, Middle, or First button.
  ➢ Change your date of birth: Click on the **Birthday** button, and then insert another date.
  ➢ Receive notifications, offers, or the Apple News newsletter: Click on **Communication Preference**. You can activate notifications; recommendations for applications, TV, songs, etc.; or subscribe to the Apple News Newsletters.

Manage your Apple ID security & password

❖ Navigate to the Settings application.
❖ Click on [Your Name], and then click on **Sign-In and Security**
  The number & e-mail address associated with your Apple ID are listed with their status.
❖ Carry out any of below:
  ➢ Delete a verified e-mail address: Click on the e-mail address, and then click on the **Remove E-mail Address** button.
  ➢ Add an e-mail address & phone number: Click on Add an E-mail or Phone Number, select Add email address or phone number, click on the **Next** button, insert the info, and then click on the **Done** button.
  ➢ Change your password: Click on the **Change Password** button, and then adhere to the directives on your display.
  ➢ Change or add a trusted phone number: Click on the **Two-Factor Authentication** button, touch your trusted phone number, verify when asked to, and then click on the **Remove Phone Number** button—if you only have one trusted number, you need to add a new one before you can remove your

current one. To add another trusted number, simply click on the **Add a Trusted Number** button.

➢ Receive a verification code to log in to iCloud.com or another device: Click on the **Two-Factor Authentication** option, and then click on the **Get Verification Code** button.

➢ Hide your e-mail address: Click on the **Forward To** button, and then select any of the addresses.

This option will allow applications to contact you without storing your real e-mail address. After selecting this option, Apple will create a random, unique e-mail address for you, & any e-mail sent from the application to this address will be forwarded to the address you pick.

View & manage your subscriptions

❖ Navigate the Settings application.
❖ Click on [your name].
❖ Click on the **Subscriptions** button, and then scroll down to view your subscriptions.
❖ Click on one of the subscriptions to view and change its options.

❖ Click on the **Cancel Subscription** button to end the subscription.

To re-subscribe to a subscription that has expired, simply touch it and then select one of the subscription options like yearly or monthly.

View & manage your devices

❖ Navigate to the Settings application.
❖ Click on [your name].
❖ Scroll down, and then click on one of the devices to show info about it.
❖ If you do not recognize the device, click on Remove from Account.

Setup the Handwashing feature

Your watch can detect when you're about to start washing your hands and advise you to continue for twenty seconds, which is the recommended time by the World Health Organization.

Activate the Handwashing feature

❖ Navigate to the Settings application.
❖ Click on the **Handwashing** button, and then activate **Handwashing Timer**.

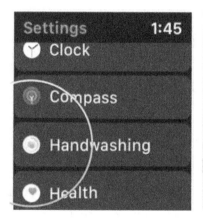 

When your smartwatch notices that you have started washing your hands, it'll start a 20-second timer. If you stop washing in less than twenty seconds, you are encouraged to complete the activity.

To view a report of your approximate handwashing time, simply enter the Health application on your phone, head over to Browse> Other Data, then click on the Handwashing button.

Connect your smartwatch to a WiFi

Connecting your smartwatch to Wifi, allows you to use many of its features even when you're not with your iPhone.

Select a WiFi network

❖ Press your watch's side button to enter the Controls Center

❖ Long-press the WiFi button 📶 , then click on any of the available WiFi networks.

❖ If a password is required before you can connect to a network, carry out any of the below:

  ➢ Use the keyboard on your watch to type the passcode.

  ➢ Touch the Password icon 🔑 , and then select any of the passwords from the list.

  ➢ Use your iPhone's keyboard to type the password.

❖ Click on the **Join** button.

Forget a network

❖ Press your watch's side button to enter the Controls Center
❖ Long-press the WiFi button 🛜, then click on the name of the network you've connected to.
❖ Click on the **Forget This Network** button.

Connect your watch to a Bluetooth speaker or headphone

Play audio from your watch on a Bluetooth speaker or headphone.

Connect a Bluetooth headphone or speaker

Follow the directives that came with the speaker or headphone to put the device in discovery mode. Once your Bluetooth device is ready to connect, simply adhere to the directives below:

❖ Navigate to the Settings application, and then click on Bluetooth.

❖ Click on the name of the device in the list when it appears.

Or, click on the AirPlay button 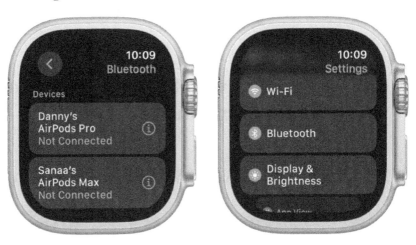 on the Play screens of the Podcasts, Now Playing, Music, & Audiobooks applications to enter the Bluetooth settings.

Select an output sound

❖ Press your watch's side button to enter the Controls Center

❖ Click on the Airplay button, and then select the device you would like to use.

Controls the volume of your headphone

❖ Press your watch's side button to enter the Controls Center
❖ Touch the Headphone Volume button  while listening to your headphone
  A meter will display the headphone's current volume.
❖ Touch the volume controls in the Headphone Volume section, and then rotate the Digital Crown to change the volume level.

Reduce loud sounds

Your smartwatch can limit your headphone's audio loudness to a certain decibel level.

❖ Enter the Settings application.
❖ Head over to Sound & Haptics> Headphones Safety, and then click on the **Reduce Loud Sounds** button.

❖ Enable **Reduce Loud Sounds**, and then select a level.

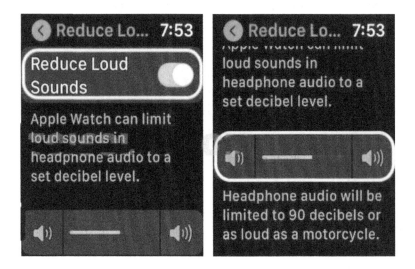

Check for loud headphone notifications

If your headphone is too loud, your smartwatch will send you an alert and automatically reduce the volume to protect your ears.

Adhere to the directives below to see information about headphone notifications:

❖ Navigate to the Settings application.
❖ Head over to Sound & Haptics> Headphones Safety, and then click on Last Six Months in the **Headphone Notifications** segment.

Or, launch the Health application on your phone, click on the **Browse** button, click on **Hearing**, touch Headphone Notifications, and then click on one of the notifications.

Handoff

The Hand-off feature allows you to switch from one Apple device to another without losing focus on what you are working on. For instance, you can start replying to an e-mail in the Mail application on your watch and finish replying to the email on your iPhone. Adhere to the directives below to use the Handoff feature.

❖ Unlock your phone.
❖ On a Face ID iPhone, swipe up from the lower edge of your display & pause to reveal the Apps Switcher.
On a Home button iPhone, press the Home button twice quickly to display the Apps Switcher.
❖ Touch the button in the lower part of the Apps Switcher on your iPhone to continue working on the application.

Tip: If you cannot find the button in the App Switcher, ensure you turn on the **Handoff** feature for your phone in the Settings application> General> AirPlay and Handoff.

Handoff is activated by default on your watch. To deactivate Handoff, simply enter the Watch application on your phone, click on the **My Watch** button, click on the **General** button, and then deactivate the **Enable Handoff** feature.

Unlock your Mac with your watch

If you have a Mac that is running macOS 10.130 or after, you can use your watch to unlock it when it wakes from sleep.

Enable the Auto-Unlock feature

* Ensure the devices are configured as follows:
  * WiFi & Bluetooth have been activated on your Mac.
  * Your smartwatch is making use of a passcode.
  * Both devices are signed in to iCloud with the same Apple ID, and your Apple ID is making use of 2-factor authentication.
* Carry out any of the below:
  * If your Mac is running macOS 13.0 or after, select Apple menu> Systems Setting, and then click on **Login Password**.
  * If your Mac is running macOS 12.0 or before, select Apple menu> Systems Preference, click on Security & Privacy, and then click on the **General** button.
* Select "**Use Apple Watch to unlock app & Mac**".

If you have multiple Apple Watches, choose the watches you want to use to unlock applications & your MacOS device.

If your Apple ID doesn't have 2-factor authentication, simply adhere to the directives on your screen, and then try to select the checkbox one more time.

Unlock your MacOS device

While putting on your smartwatch, simply wake your Mac—you don't have to enter your password.

Tip: To unlock your Mac, ensure your smartwatch is on your wrist, unlocked, and close to your Mac.

Unlock your iPhone with your smartwatch

You can use your smartwatch to unlock your phone if an obstruction is preventing Face ID from recognizing your face. To do this, simply adhere to the directives below:

❖ Enter the Settings application on your iPhone, touch Face ID and Passcode, and then insert your iPhone passcode.
❖ Scroll down to the **Unlock With Apple Watch** section, and then activate the feature for your smartwatch.

If you have multiple watches, activate the feature for each of them.

❖ To unlock your phone, make sure you are putting on your smartwatch, wake your phone, and then stare at your iPhone's screen.

Your smartwatch will tap your wrist to inform you that your phone has been unlocked.

Tip: To unlock your iPhone, ensure your smartwatch is on your wrist, unlocked, and close to your phone.

Setup & make use of cellular services on your smartwatch

With a mobile connection to the carrier used by your phone, you can reply to messages, make calls, stream songs, & more, even when you are not with your iPhone or connected to a WiFi network.

Add your watch to your mobile plan

You can activate mobile service on your smartwatch by adhering to the onscreen directives during initial setup. To activate it later, simply adhere to the directives below:

* ❖ Enter the Watch application on your phone.
* ❖ Click on the **My Watch** button, and then click on the **Cellular** button.

Adhere to the directives on your display to get more information about your carrier's service plan & activate cellular for your smartwatch. You might need to contact your carrier for help.

Transfer a cellular plan to your new smartwatch

Adhere to the directives below to transfer cellular service from your old Apple Watch to your Apple Watch Ultra:

❖ While putting on your old watch, enter the Watch application on your phone
❖ Touch the **My Watch** button, click on the **Cellular** button, and then click on the Info icon 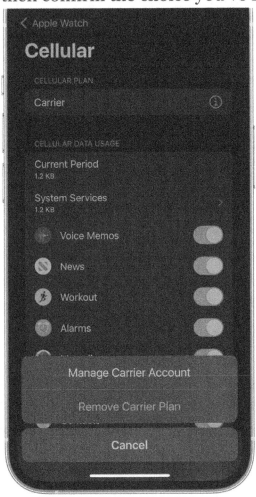 beside your cellular plan.
❖ Click on **Remove [carrier name] Plan**, and then confirm the choice you've made.

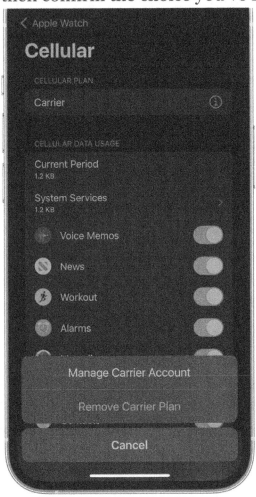

You might need to contact your carrier to remove this smartwatch from your plan

❖ Remove your old smartwatch from your wrist, wear your Apple Watch Ultra, touch the **My Watch** button in the Watch app on your phone, and then touch the **Cellular** button. Adhere to the directives on your display to activate your smartwatch for cellular.

Activate or deactivate cellular

❖ Press your watch's side button to enter the Control Centre.

❖ Click on the Cellular button ^{((ᵠ))}, and then activate or deactivate Cellular.

The Cellular button will change to green when your smartwatch has a mobile connection & your phone is not nearby.

Check mobile signal strength

Press your watch's side button to reveal the Controls Centre. The green bar in the upper part of the screen shows the mobile connection status.

Check your mobile data usage

❖ Enter the Settings application on your smartwatch.

❖ Click on the **Cellular** button, then scroll down to see how much data you have used so far.

Control your watch with your phone

The **Apple Watch Mirroring** feature allows you to control your smartwatch with your phone.

❖ Enter the Settings application on your paired iPhone.
❖ Touch Accessibility> Apple Watch Mirroring, and then activate the **Apple Watch Mirroring** feature.

An image showing your watch's screen will appear on your phone. Use the following gestures on the mirrored image.

❖ Scroll: Swipe the screen down or up.
❖ Move from one screen to another: Swipe the screen right or left.
❖ Press the Digital Crown: Touch the Digital Crown on your phone screen.
❖ Press the side button: Touch the side button on your phone screen
❖ Use Siri: Long-press the Digital Crown on your phone screen.

Control Apple devices close to you with your smartwatch

You can use your watch to control your iPad or iPhone.

❖ Enter the Settings application on your smartwatch.
❖ Head over to Accessibility> Control Nearby Device

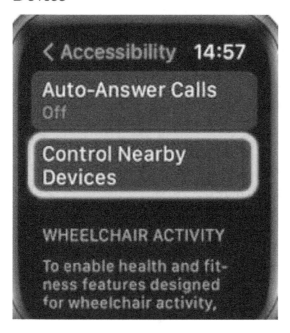

Your iPad or iPhone has to be logged in to iCloud with the same Apple ID as your watch & both devices must be on the same network.

❖ Select one of the devices if there are multiple devices nearby, and then touch a button.

The buttons replicate the controls on your device and include:

- Apps Switcher
- Notification Center
- Home button
- Siri
- Controls Centre
- Options (includes customizable hand gestures & media play controls)

AssistiveTouch

The AssistiveTouch feature can help you use your smartwatch if you have trouble touching the display or pressing buttons. The sensors built into your smartwatch can help you answer calls, launch an actions menu, and more—with hand gestures.

With AssistiveTouch, you can perform the following actions with hand gestures:

- ❖ Tap your screen
- ❖ Swipe from one screen to another
- ❖ Use Apple Pay
- ❖ Press & rotate the Digital Crown
- ❖ Access the Apps Switcher, Controls Centre, & Notifications Centre
- ❖ Long-press the side button
- ❖ Show applications
- ❖ Activate Siri
- ❖ And more

Setup AssistiveTouch

❖ Enter the Settings application on your smartwatch.

❖ Head over to Accessibility

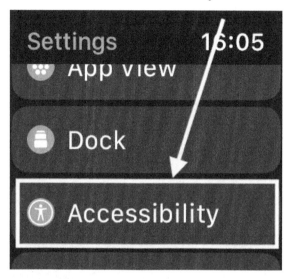

❖ Click on AssistiveTouch, and then activate AssistiveTouch.

❖ Touch the **Hand Gestures** button, and then activate Hand Gestures

Tip: To get more info about how to make use of hand gestures, simply click on **Learn More** under the **Hand Gesture** switch, and then click on each gesture. After tapping on a gesture, you'll see an interactive animation on your screen that will show you how to perform the gesture.

You can also enter the Watch application on your phone, click on the My Watch button in the lower part of your display, head over to Accessibility, click on AssistiveTouch, and then enable **AssistiveTouch**.

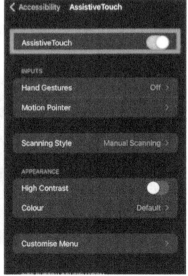

Use AssistiveTouch with your watch

After activating the AssistiveTouch & Hand Gestures feature, navigate through your watch with the following gestures:

❖ Clench: Touch or Tap

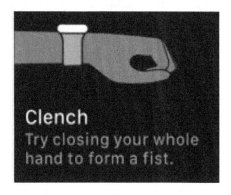

❖ Clench twice: Display the Actions Menu
❖ Pinch: Forward

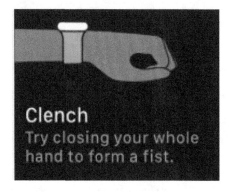

❖ Pinch twice: Back

For instance, with the Meridian watch face showing, use the AssistiveTouch feature with the Activity application by adhering to the directives below:

- ❖ Clench twice quickly to activate the **AssistiveTouch** feature.
  You'll see a highlight around the Music complication
- ❖ Pinch thrice to go to the Activity complication, and then clench once to touch the complication.
- ❖ After the Activity application opens, clench twice to bring the Actions Menu out.
- ❖ Pinch to highlight the Systems action, pinch one more time to highlight the Scroll Up action, and then clench once to choose it.
- ❖ Clench once to go to the next screen
- ❖ Pinch-twice quickly to display the Actions Menu
  Pinch once to go forward through the actions; pinch twice to go back.
- ❖ Select the Press Crown action, and then clench to go back to the watch face.

Use the Motion Pointer

The Motion Pointer feature allows you to control your smartwatch by tilting the watch down & up and side to side. For instance, use Motion Pointer to surf through the Stopwatch application by adhering to the directives below:

❖ With one of the watch faces showing, clench twice to activate the **AssistiveTouch** feature.

❖ Clench twice again to bring the Actions Menu out.
  Your watch will select the Press Crown action.
❖ Clench once to choose the Press Crown action & open your smartwatch Home screen
❖ Clench twice to bring the Actions Menu out, pinch to go to the Interactions action, and then clench to touch it.
  The Motions Pointer should be highlighted
❖ Clench to activate the Motion Pointer

You'll see a cursor on your screen

❖ Tilt your smartwatch to move the cursor to the lower edge of your display to scroll down.
❖ Hold the cursor over the Stopwatch application for a few seconds to launch the application
❖ Hold the cursor over the **Start** key to touch it.
❖ To go back to the watch face, clench twice to display the Actions Menu, pinch to highlight the Press Crown action, and then clench to touch it.

Use quick actions

The Quick Action feature helps you respond when your smartwatch displays an alert. For instance, if someone calls you, a prompt will inform you that you can pinch twice to answer the call. You can also use quick actions to stop a timer, snooze an alarm, and more. Adhere to the directives below to activate or deactivate quick actions.

❖ Enter the Settings application on your smartwatch.
❖ Head over to Accessibility, touch Quick Actions, and then pick any of the options.

Tip: Click on the **Try it out** button to learn how to perform quick action gestures.

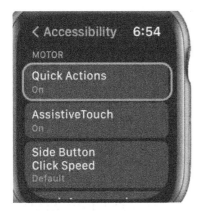

Change AssistiveTouch settings

Enter the Settings application, head over to Accessibility, touch the **AssistiveTouch** button, and then carry out any of the below:

❖ Personalize gestures: Click on the **Hand Gestures** button, select one of the gestures, and then pick one of the actions or Siri shortcuts.

❖ Personalize the Motion Pointer: Click Motions Pointer, and then change the settings for hot edges, movement tolerance, activation time, & sensitivity.

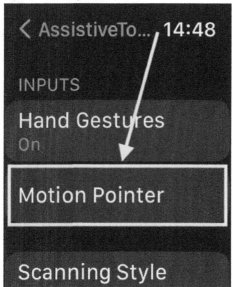

❖ Scanning style: Pick a scanning style (Manual or Auto). The Auto Scanning style helps your smartwatch to automatically highlight actions one after the other, while in Manual mode, you have to use gestures to switch from one gesture to another.

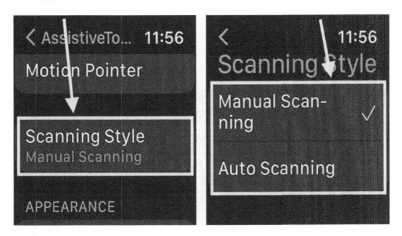

❖ Appearance: Enable High Contrast to enhance features. Touch the **Colour** button to select a new highlight colour.

❖ Personalize Menu: Add favourite actions, change the size & position of the Actions Menu, & adjust the speed of autoscroll.

❖ Confirm with AssistiveTouch: Activate this setting to be able to use AssistiveTouch to verify payment with the password or whenever double-pressing the side button is a requirement.

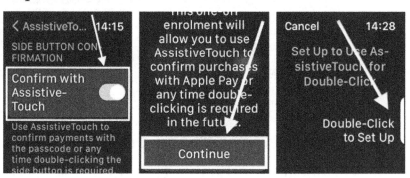

Or, enter the Watch application on your phone, touch the **My Watch** button, and then Head over to Accessibility > AssistiveTouch.

Use Zoom

Use the **Zoom** feature to make items on your screen bigger.

Activate Zoom

❖ Navigate to the Settings application.
❖ Head over to Accessibility, and touch Zoom

❖ Enable the **Zoom** feature.

Or, enter the Watch application on your phone, touch the **My Watch** button, touch Accessibility, and then click on Zoom.

Control Zoom

After activating Zoom, you can carry out the following actions on your smartwatch.

* Zoom out or in: Use 2 of your fingers to double-tap your watch screen.
* Pan: Use 2 of your fingers to drag the screen. Or, roll the Digital Crown to pan over the whole page, up-down & left-right. A small Zoom button will appear to show you where you are on the page.
* Use the Digital Crown for its normal function instead of panning: Tap your watch screen with 2 of your fingers to switch between using the Digital Crown to move around the screen & using it for its normal function (for instance, scrolling through a list or zooming in on a map).
* Adjust zoom: Double-tap & hold with 2 of your fingers, and then drag your fingers down or up on your screen. To limit magnification, touch the minus or plus button in the Maximum Zoom Level slider.

Live Speech

With the Live Speech feature, you can type & have your words spoken out loud, both in person or in calls.

Setup Live Speech

* ❖ Navigate to the Settings application on your smartwatch.
* ❖ Click on Accessibility, tap Live Speech, and then touch Voices.
* ❖ Pick one of the voices, and the touch Speak Sample to listen to it.
  To make use of the voice, click on Download [Voice name], and then click on the **Use Voice** button.
* ❖ To setup the Accessibility Shortcut to activate Live Speech, simply enter the Settings application, tap Accessibility, tap Accessibility Shortcut, and then select Live Speech.

Type to speak

* ❖ Click the Digital Crown three times, and then type what you would like to have spoken or select one of your favourite phrases.
  Tip: Add your most used phrases for quick access to them. Navigate to the Settings

application, touch Accessibility, touch Live Speech, and then click on Favourite Phrases.

❖ Click on the **Speak** button to speak the phrase you typed or selected.

If you are on a call, people on the call will hear your words spoken in the conversation. Otherwise, they'll come out of your watch's speaker.

Set Alarm

❖ Navigate to the Alarms application on your smartwatch.

❖ Click on the **Add Alarm** icon .

❖ Click on PM or AM, and then click on the minutes or hours.
This step is not necessary when making use of a 24-hour time.

❖ Rotate the Digital Crown to adjust, then click on the Done icon .

❖ To activate or deactivate the alarm, touch its switch. Or touch the alarm time to set snooze, label, & repeat options.

Turn off snooze

When an alarm starts playing, you can click on the **Snooze** button to wait a few minutes before the alarm starts playing again.

Adhere to the directives below to deactivate the Snooze feature:

❖ Launch the Alarms application on your smartwatch.
❖ Click on the alarm in the alarms list, and then deactivate the **Snooze** feature.

Delete an alarm

❖ Launch the Alarms application on your smartwatch.
❖ Click on the alarm in the alarms list.
❖ Scroll down, and then click on the **Delete** button.

Skip a wake-up alarm

If you set a wake-up alarm that is part of your sleep routine, you can skip the alarm for a day.

❖ Launch the Alarms application on your smartwatch.
❖ Click on the alarm under Alarms, and then click on **Skip for Tonight**.

See the same alarms on your iPhone & smartwatch

❖ Set the alarm on your phone.
❖ Navigate to the Watch application on your phone
❖ Click on the **My Watch** button, click on the **Clock** button, and then activate the **Push Alerts from iPhone** feature.

Turn your smartwatch into a nightstand watch with alarm

❖ Navigate to the Settings application on your watch.
❖ Head over to General, touch Nightstand Mode, and then enable Nightstand Mode.

When your watch is connected to its charger while nightstand mode is enabled, it'll show the charging status, current date & time, and the alarm time you've set on the screen. Touch the screen or lightly nudge your watch to see the time.

If you set an alarm, your watch in Nightstand Mode will gently wake you up. When the alarm starts playing, press the side button to turn off the alarm, or press the Digital Crown for Snooze to give yourself a few minutes to rest.

Perform a quick calculation

❖ Launch the Calculator application  on your smartwatch.
❖ Touch the numbers & operators to get answers.

Split the check and calculate a tip

- ❖ Launch the Calculator application on your smartwatch.
- ❖ Enter the total bill, then touch the **Tip** button.

- ❖ Rotate the Digital Crown to select the tip percentage.
- ❖ Click on **People**, and then rotate the Digital Crown to select the number of individuals that want to share the bill.

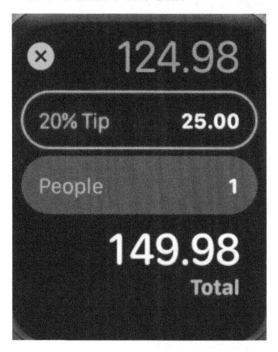

You'll see the total amount, the tip, and how much each individual is supposed to pay.

Check the time in other places on your smartwatch

You can check the time in other cities around the world in the World Clock application ⊕ .

Add & remove cities in World Clock

- ❖ Launch the World Clock application ⊕ .
- ❖ Click on the List icon ⊜ , and then click the Add icon ⊕ .
- ❖ Type the name of the city, or use dictation to enter the name of the city.
- ❖ Touch the name of the city to add it to the World Clock application.

To remove a city, simply swipe left on the name of the city, and then touch the **X** button.

Check the time in other cities

- ❖ Launch the World Clock application ⊕ .
- ❖ Click on the List icon ⊜ , and then rotate the Digital Crown to scroll down
- ❖ To get more info about a city, including its sunrise & sunset times, simply touch the city in the list

❖ When you are done, touch the Back icon to go back to the cities list.

Change the city abbreviations

❖ Launch the Watch application on your phone
❖ Click on the **My Watch** button, touch Clock, and then touch City Abbreviations
❖ Touch one of the cities to change its abbreviation.

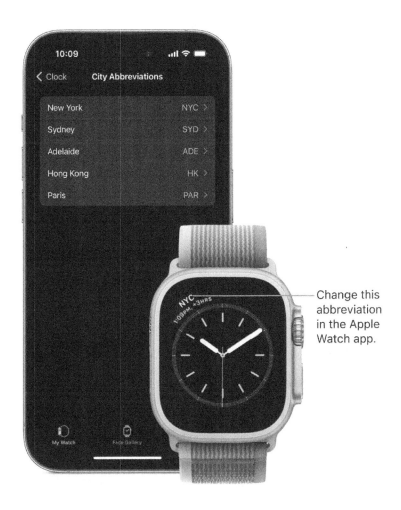

Change this abbreviation in the Apple Watch app.

Time events with stopwatch

Time events with accuracy and keep track of split or lap times in the Stopwatch application.

Choose a Stopwatch

❖ Launch the Stopwatch application .
❖ Rotate the Digital Crown to select a different format.
   You can pick Digital, Hybrid, or Analog.

Start, stop & reset the stopwatch

Launch the Stopwatch application, rotate the Digital Crown to select one of the formats, and then carry out any of the below:

❖ Start: Touch the Start icon ▶.
❖ Record a lap: Click on the Lap icon ●.
❖ Record the final time: Click on the Stop button ■.
❖ When the stopwatch stops, click on the Reset icon ⊜ to reset the stopwatch.

The stopwatch will keep counting even if you go to the watch face or launch other applications.

Start or stop the stopwatch.

Record lap times.

SAFETY FEATURES

Your watch can be useful in emergency situations.

Setup & view your Medical ID

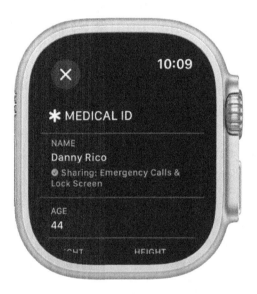

Your Medical ID contains your information that can be important in emergency situations, such as health conditions & allergies. When you setup your Medical ID in the Health application on your phone, that info will become available on your watch. If you share your medical ID, your watch can send your medical info to the emergency department when you make use of Emergency SOS or contact 911.

Your smartwatch can display your Medical ID so that the person who's attending to you in an emergency can see it.

Follow the directives below to view your Medical ID on your watch:

❖ Hold down the side button till you see the sliders
❖ Drag the Medical ID slider to the right end of your display
❖ Click on the **Done** button when you are done.

Or, navigate to the Settings application on your smartwatch, then head over to SOS>Medical ID.

Setup Medical ID & add emergency contacts

❖ Navigate to the Settings application on your phone, touch Health, and then click on Medical ID
❖ Touch the **Create Medical ID** button or the **Edit** button.
❖ Insert your birthdate & other health info.

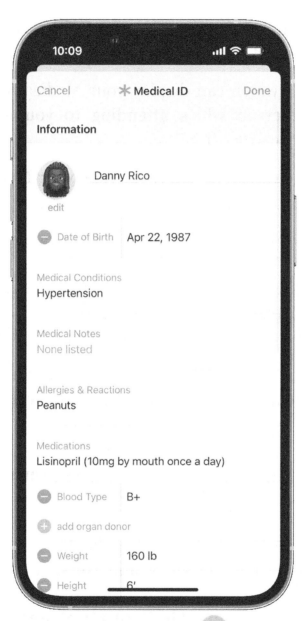

❖ Click on the Add icon 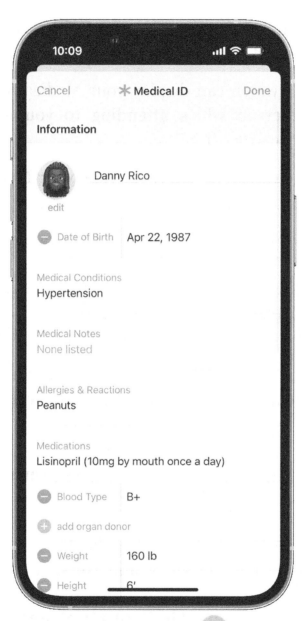 in the Emergency Contacts segment to add emergency contacts.

Click on a contact, and then add the contact's relationship to you.

❖ To remove a contact, simply click on the Remove icon ⬤ beside the contact and then click on **Delete**.

❖ Activate the **Show When Locked** feature to make your health info accessible from the lock screen. In an emergency situation, this provides info to people who want to help. Activate the **Share during Emergency Call** option to share your health information with emergency personnel. When you call or text emergency services on your iPhone or smartwatch, your Medical ID will be automatically shared with the emergency department.

❖ Touch **Done.**

Contact emergency services with your smartwatch

Use your watch to call for help in an emergency.

Contact emergency services

Carry out any of the below:

❖ Long-press your watch's side button till you see the sliders, and then drag the Emergency Call slider to the right end of your display.

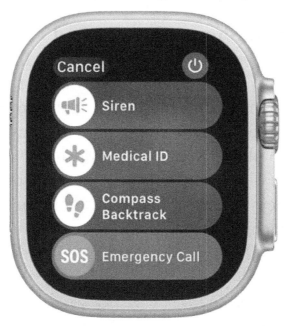

Your smartwatch will call the emergency department in your area, such as 911 (In some areas, you may have to press a number on the keypad to complete the call.)

❖ Press & hold the Side button till your watch plays a warning sound & begins a countdown. After the countdown, your smartwatch will call the emergency department.

Your smartwatch will make a warning sound even if it is in silent mode, so if you are in a situation where you do not want to make noise, simply make use of the Emergency Call slider to contact the emergency department.

You can deactivate the **Automatic Dialing** feature if you do not want your smartwatch to automatically begin the emergency countdown when you long-press the side button. To do this, simply enter the Settings application on your watch, touch SOS, touch **Hold Side Button**, and then deactivate the **Hold Side Button** feature. (Or, enter the Watch application on your phone, click on the **My Watch** tab, click on the **Emergency SOS** button, and then deactivate Hold Side Button To Dial). You can still use the Emergency Call Slider to contact emergency services.

❖ Enter the Message application on your watch, touch the **New Message** button, touch the **Add Contacts** button, click on the number pad button, and then write 911. Touch the **Create Message** button, type your message, and then click on the **Send** button.

❖ Say "Hey Siri, call 911."

Cancel an emergency call

If you mistakenly start an emergency call, simply click on the End Call icon , and then click on the **End Call** button to cancel the call.

Change your emergency address

If the emergency services cannot find you, they'll go to your emergency address.

❖ Navigate to the Settings application on your phone.
❖ Scroll down, touch Phone, touch WiFi Calling, touch Update Emergency Address, and then fill in your emergency address.

Turn on the siren

Your smartwatch has an inbuilt siren that emits a powerful sound. With the siren, you can try to attract help in an emergency situation.

Carry out any of the below to activate the siren:

❖ Long-press the Action button, and then wait for your watch to finish the countdown.

Touch the **Cancel** button to stop the siren from playing.

Note: To stop the siren from playing when you long-press the Action button, enter the Settings application on your smartwatch, click on Action button, and then deactivate **Hold to Turn On** under the Sirens heading

❖ Long-press your watch's side button, and then slide the Siren slider to the right end of your display.

❖ Enter the Siren application on your smartwatch, and then touch the Play icon ▶.
❖ Say " Start the siren," and then touch the Play icon ▶

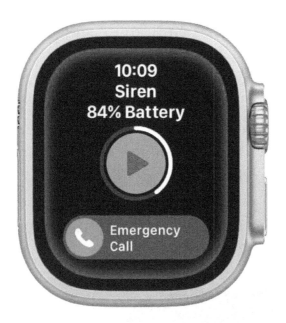

Your smartwatch will continue to play the siren & tap your wrist till you deactivate Siren or your watch battery runs out of power.

WARNING: If possible, don't activate the siren near your ear or in an enclosed place.

Fall Detection

With the **Fall Detection** feature activated, your smartwatch can help you contact emergency services & send messages to your emergency contacts if it notices a hard fall. If your smartwatch detects a hard fall and you've not moved for a minute, it will tap your wrist, play a sound, and then try to contact the emergency department.

To contact the emergency department, your smartwatch or iPhone needs a mobile connection.

If there is no cellular coverage and your iPhone 14 or later is close to your watch, Fall Detection will use your iPhone to send the notification using Emergency SOS via satellite.

If the date of birth you entered when setting up your smartwatch or the one you added in the Health application on your phone indicates that you are more than 55 years old, the Fall Detection feature is automatically activated on your device. If you are between the ages of 18 & 55, you can activate the Fall Detection feature by adhering to the directives below:

* Navigate to the Settings applications.
* Head over to SOS> Fall Detections, and then activate the **Fall Detection** feature.
  Or, enter the Watch application on your phone, click on the **My Watch** tab, click on Emergency SOS, and then enable the **Fall Detection** feature.
  Note: If you deactivate wrist detection, your smartwatch will not automatically try to contact emergency services even after detecting a hard fall.
* Select the **"Always On"** option to have the Fall Detections feature active every time, or the **Only on During Workouts** feature to have it active only when you are working out.

Crash Detection

Your smartwatch can help you contact the emergency department & send messages to your emergency contacts if it detects that you've been in a serious car accident.

When your smartwatch detects a serious car accident, it'll show a notification and start an emergency phone call after twenty seconds unless it's canceled. If you're unresponsive, your smartwatch will send a voice message to the emergency services, informing them that you've been involved in a car accident. It'll also send your location details to the emergency department.

To contact the emergency department, your smartwatch or iPhone needs a mobile connection.

If there's no cellular coverage and your iPhone 14 or after is close to your smartwatch, the emergency department can be notified via the Emergency SOS satellite network if it's available.

Enable or disable Crash Detection

* Navigate to the Settings application on your smartwatch.
* Head over to SOS> Crash Detections, and then disable **Call After Severe Crash**.

SIRI

With Siri's help, you can perform tasks & receive answers to questions on your watch. You can tell Siri to help you to translate a phrase, set an alarm, find a place, etc.

Setup Siri

Navigate to the Settings application on your watch, click on Siri, and then enable the Raise to

Speak, Listen for Siri or Hey Siri, and the Press Digital Crown features.

How to make use of Siri

Carry out any of the below to summon Siri and make a request:

❖ Lift your wrist to your mouth level and speak into your smartwatch.
To deactivate this feature, navigate to the Settings application on your smartwatch, click on the **Siri** button, and then deactivate the **Raise to Speak** feature.

❖ Say "Siri" or "Hey Siri" and then ask a question or request for something.
To deactivate this feature, navigate to the Settings application, click on Siri, click on Listen for "Hey Siri" or "Siri," and then select the **Off** option.

❖ Hold down the Digital Crown till the listening indicator appears on your screen, and then ask for something.
To disable this feature, simply navigate to the Settings application on your smartwatch, click

on Siri, and then deactivate the **Press Digital Crown** feature.

Tip: After activating Siri and making a request, you can put your hand down. Your smartwatch will tap you when there is a response.

To answer Siri's question or continue the conversation, simply long-press the Digital Crown & talk

Note: To use Siri, your smartwatch has to have an internet connection.

Choose how Siri responds

Navigate to the Settings application, click on **Siri**, click on Siri Response, and then select from the below:

❖ Control in silent mode: Siri's responses will be silenced when you put your smartwatch in silent mode.
❖ Always on: Siri will speak responses, even when you put your watch in silent mode.
❖ Headphone only: Siri will only speak responses when you connect your smartwatch to a Bluetooth headphone.

To change Siri's voice & language, navigate to the Settings application, click on the **Siri** button, and then click on Siri's Voice or Language. After tapping Siri Voice, you can now pick from the different options.

Show captions & your Siri requests transcriptions

Your watch can show Siri captions & transcription for Siri requests & Siri response. To change any of the options, navigate to the Settings application, click on the **Siri** button, click on Siri Response, scroll, and then enable or disable Always Show Siri Caption & Always Show Speech.

Type to Siri & Siri Pause Time

The **Type to Siri** feature allows you to use Siri without speaking. Follow the directions below to type your request instead of speaking it.

❖ Navigate to the Settings application on your smartwatch.

❖ Head over to Accessibility, click on Siri, and then enable the **Type to Siri** feature.

Set how long you want Siri to wait for you to finish speaking

❖ Navigate to the Settings application on your smartwatch.
❖ Head over to Accessibility, click on Siri, scroll down, and then select Longest or Longer in the **Siri Pause Time** section.

Delete Siri's history

Your Siri requests are stored on Apple's server for 6 months to make Siri's responses to you better. You can erase these requests from Apple's server anytime you like.

❖ Navigate to the Settings application on your smartwatch
❖ Click on the **Siri** button, click on Siri History, and then click on Delete Siri History

Announce Notifications

The **Announce Notifications** feature allows Siri to read out incoming notifications from many applications when your smartwatch is connected to supported Airpods & headphones.

❖ Pair your headphone with your Apple watch and put it on.
❖ Navigate to the Settings application on your smartwatch.
❖ Head over to Siri> Announce Notification, and then enable the **Announce Notification** feature.

Or, launch the Settings application on your phone, head over to Notification> Announce Notification, and then enable the **Announce Notification** feature.

Tip: You can also tell Siri to help you read out your unread notifications in the Notifications Centre—either through your watch's speaker or headphones connected to your smartwatch. To do this, simply say **"Read my notifications "**.

Select applications for notification

You can select which applications are allowed to use the Announce Notifications feature.

❖ Put on your connected headphones
❖ Navigate to the Settings application.
❖ Head over to Siri> Announce Notification, scroll down, and then select the apps.

Temporarily deactivate the Announce Notifications feature

❖ Press your watch's side button to enter the Controls Center
❖ Tap on the Announce Notification button

Tap the Announce Notifications button one more time to activate it.

Reply to a message

You could say, "Reply that's good to know."

Siri will repeat what you said, and then ask you to confirm your reply before sending it. (To send replies without asking for confirmation, navigate to the Settings application on your smartwatch, head over to Siri> Announce Notifications, scroll down, and then activate the **Reply without Confirmation** feature.)

Stop Siri from reading a notification

Carry out any of the below:

❖ You could say **Cancel** or **Stop.**
❖ Press the Digital Crown.
❖ Double tap one of the AirPods
❖ Press the Force Sensor on the AirPod

Announce calls

The Announce Calls feature allows Siri to identify incoming calls, which you can accept or decline with your voice.

❖ Navigate to the Settings application on your smartwatch.
❖ Click on the **Siri** button, and then enable the **Announce Calls** feature.
❖ When someone calls you, your smartwatch will identify the caller and ask if you would like to take the call. You can either say Yes to take the call or No to decline it.

WATCH FACES

Your watch comes with a collection of watch faces that can be personalized to suit your style.

Tap the watch face, then turn to move forward or back in time.

Visit the Apple Watch face gallery

You'll find all your Apple Watch faces in the Face gallery on your iPhone. When you see a watch face you like, you can personalize it, pick complications, and then add it to your collection— all from the face gallery.

Open the Face Gallery

Launch the Watch application on your phone, and then click on the **Face Gallery** button at the bottom of your display.

Select features for a watch face

Touch any of the watch faces in the Face gallery, and then click on any of the features such as style or colour.

As you select different options, the face in the upper part of your screen will change to ensure the design is perfect.

Add complications

❖ Touch one of the watch faces in the Face gallery, and then select one of the complication positions, like Bottom Right, or Bottom Left.

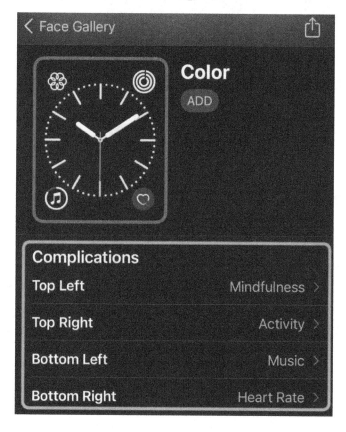

❖ Swipe to view all available complications for the position you selected, and then select the complication you like.
❖ If you decide you do not want the position to have any complication, simply scroll up to the beginning of the list and then click on **Off**.

Add a face

❖ Touch one of the faces in the Face gallery, and then select the complications & features you like.
❖ Touch the **Add** button.

The watch face will be added to your collection & it'll become the current face on your smartwatch.

Personalize the watch face

You can personalize your watch face—right on your Apple Watch—to look the way you like & give you the features you want.

Pick another watch face

Long-press the watch face, swipe to the face you like, and touch it.

Swipe left or right to see other watch faces.

Add features to your watch face.

Add a complication to the watch face

You can add features known as complications to many Apple watch faces, so that you can easily check things like the price of a stock, weather forecast, etc.

- ❖ With the watch face showing, press & hold the screen, and then touch the **Edit** button.
- ❖ Swipe left continuously till you reach the end. If a watch face has complications, you will see them on the last screen.
- ❖ Click on any of the complications to select it, and then rotate the Digital Crown to pick another complication—like Workout or Music.

Turn to scroll through options.

- ❖ When you are done, press the Digital Crown to store the changes you have made, and then touch the face to use it.

Add a watch face to your collection

Create your collection of customized watch faces, even different versions of the same design.

- ❖ With the watch face showing, long-press the screen.
- ❖ Swipe left continuously till you reach the end, and then click on the Add icon (+).
- ❖ Roll the Digital Crown to see the watch faces, and then click on the **Add** button.
  Tip: Touch one of the collections (for example, Artists) to view a specific category of watch faces.

After adding it, you can personalize the watch face.

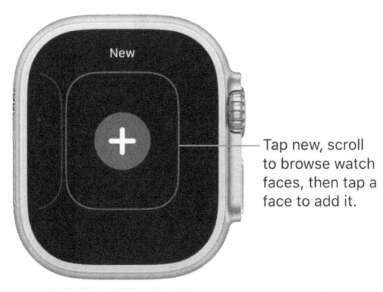

Tap new, scroll to browse watch faces, then tap a face to add it.

View your collection

You can view all your watch faces in one place.

❖ Navigate to the Watch application on your phone.
❖ Click on the **My Watch** button in the lower part of your display, and then swipe to see your collection under **My Faces**.

To reorder your collection, click on the **Edit** button in the **My Faces** section, then drag the Rearrange icon ▬ beside a watch face down or up.

Delete a watch face from your collection

❖ With the watch face showing, long-press your screen.
❖ Swipe to the watch face you plan on deleting, swipe the watch face up, and then click on **Remove**.

Or, launch the Watch application on your phone, click on the **My Watch** tab in the lower part of your display, and then click on the **Edit** button in the My Faces section. Touch the Delete icon ⊖ beside a watch face, and then click on **Remove**.

Swipe up to delete a watch face, then tap Remove.

Set the watch ahead

❖ Navigate to the Settings application.
❖ Touch the **Clock** button
❖ Click on the +0 min, and then roll the Digital Crown to set the watch ahead.

This setting will only change the time displayed on your watch face—it does not have any effect on alarms, notifications, or other times (like the World Clock).

Share Apple Watch faces

You can share watch faces with others.

❖ With the watch face showing on your Apple Watch, long-press the screen, and then click on the Share icon ⬆.

❖ Click on the watch face's name, and then touch the **Don't include** button for the complications you do not want to share.

❖ Click on one of the recipients, or click Mail or Message
If you select Mail or Message, add a contact & message

❖ Click on the **Send** button.

Or, launch the Watch application on your phone, click on one of the watch faces from the Face Gallery or your collection, click on the Share button ⬆️, and then pick any of the sharing options.

Receive a watch face

❖ Open an e-mail, text, or link that contains the watch face that was sent to you.
❖ Click on the watch face, and then click on **Add**.

Create a photo watch face

While viewing a picture in the Photos application ✳️ , touch the Share button ⬆️, scroll down, and then touch the **Create Face** button.

ACTIVITY

The Activity application tracks your movement for the whole day & motivates you to reach your fitness target. The application keeps track of how long you exercise, how much you move, & how often you stand. 3 different colored rings summarize your progress. The goal is to complete each ring every day by exercising, moving more, & sitting less.

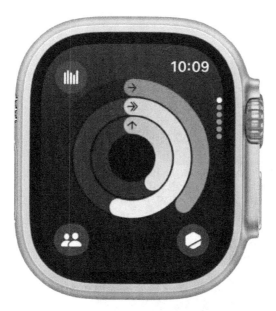

The Fitness application on your iPhone records your activity. If you have tracked activity for a minimum of six months, the Fitness application will display daily trend data for stand hours, active calories, walking pace, walk distance, stand minutes, cardio fitness, etc. In the Fitness application on your phone, click on the **Summary** button, and then go to Trends to check how you are doing compared to your usual activity.

Set up the Activity app

When setting up your smartwatch, you are asked if you would like to setup the Activity application. If you did not configure it during the Apple Watch setup, you can do it later when you enter the application for the 1st time.

* Launch the Activity application
* Use the Digital Crown to read the Stand, Workout, & Move description, and then click on the **Get Started** button

View your progress

Enter the Activity application at any time to check your progress. The application shows 3 rings.

* The red activity ring (also known as the Move ring) shows the amount of calories you have burned.
* The blue activity ring (also known as the Stand ring) shows how many minutes you have moved & stood for a minimum of 1 minute per hour.

❖ The green activity ring (also known as the Exercise ring) displays how many minutes of brisk activity you have done.

If you indicated that you are a wheelchair user, the blue Stand ring will become the Roll ring & it will show how many times you have rolled for a minimum of 1 minute per hour.

Roll the Digital Crown to check your current total—continue scrolling to view your progress for each ring, your activity history, flights climbed, total distance, & total steps.

When a ring overlaps, it means that you've exceeded your target. Touch the Weekly Summary icon ⬤ to view your progress for the week.

Change your goals

If you feel that your activity goals are too difficult or too easy, you can change them.

❖ Enter the Activity application
❖ Touch the Weekly Summary icon ⬤
❖ Roll the Digital Crown to scroll down, and then touch the **Change Goals** button.
❖ Click on the Minus icon ⬤ or the Add icon ⊕ to change a target, and then click on the **Next** button.
❖ When you are done, touch **OK**

To change targets for each ring, rotate the Digital Crown to a goal, and then touch the Change Targets icon ⬤.

Every Monday, you will be informed of the achievements of the previous week and you can adjust your goals for the following week.

View your activity history

❖ Launch the Fitness application on your phone, and then click on the **Summary** button.
❖ Click on the Activity area, click on the Calendar

icon   ⸗, and click on a date.

Check your trends

In the Fitness application on your phone, the Trends section shows you daily trend data for running pace, walking pace, cardio fitness, standing minutes, walking distance, stand hours, exercise minutes, & active calories.

Adhere to the directives below to find out more:

❖ Launch the Fitness application on your iPhone.
❖ In the Trends section, click on the **Show More** button.
❖ Touch a trend to view its history.

Check your awards

Adhere to the directives below to view all of your activity awards:

- ❖ Enter the Activity application.
- ❖ Click on the Awards icon  .
- ❖ Touch one of the awards to get more information about it.

Control activity reminders

Reminders can help achieve goals. Your smartwatch lets you know if you are on track with your activity goals or not. Follow these steps to choose which reminders you want to see:

- ❖ Navigate to the Settings application.

❖ Click on the **Activity** button, and then configure the notifications

Suspend daily coaching

Adhere to the directives below to deactivate activity reminders:

❖ Navigate to the Settings application.
❖ Click on the **Activity** button, and then deactivate Daily Coaching.

BLOOD OXYGEN

You can use the Blood Oxygen application ◌ to measure the percentage of oxygen your red blood cells are carrying from your lungs to the other parts of your body. Having knowledge of how much oxygen your blood has can help you understand your overall health and well-being.

Note: You have to ensure your iPhone XS or after, and Apple Watch Ultra have been updated to the latest version of their operating system.

Note: The Blood Oxygen application isn't available for use by individuals under the age of 18.

Setup Blood Oxygen

❖ Enter the Settings application
❖ Click on Blood Oxygen, and then activate Blood Oxygen Measurement.

Measuring the level of oxygen in your blood

The Blood Oxygen application can measure your blood oxygen level periodically throughout the day if background measurement is activated, but you can also measure it whenever you want.

❖ Navigate to the Blood Oxygen application.
❖ Place your hand on a table or your lap and ensure your wrist is flat, with your watch's screen facing up.
❖ Touch the **Start** button, and make sure your hand is still during the countdown.

Make sure your watch is not loose or too tight on your wrist.

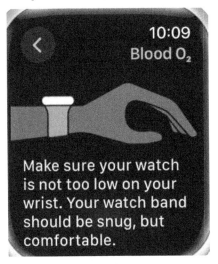

* You'll receive the results after the measurement is completed. Click on the **Done** button.

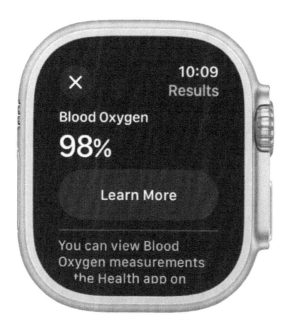

Deactivate background measurements when theater mode or the Sleep Focus is on

The blood oxygen meter uses a bright red light that shines on your wrist, making it more visible in dark areas. If the light bothers you, you can turn off the measurement.

- ❖ Navigate to the Settings application.
- ❖ Click on the **Blood Oxygen** button, and then deactivate In Theater Mode & In Sleep Focus.

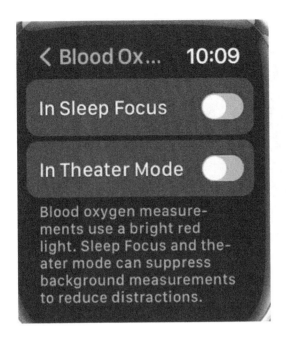

See blood oxygen measurement history

❖ Launch the Health application on your phone.
❖ Click on the **Browse** button, click on Respiratory, and then touch Blood Oxygen.

CAMERA REMOTE

You can set your iPhone for a video or picture and then use your smartwatch to capture the picture or video from a distance. By default, there is a 3-second delay before the shot is captured, giving you time to put your hand down & raise your eyes for the shot.

Your smartwatch has to be within the standard Bluetooth range of your iPhone (about 33ft) in order for the camera to work remotely.

Choose options.

Take a photo.

Take pictures

- ❖ Enter the Camera Remote application 📷 on your smartwatch.
- ❖ Set up your phone to frame the shot using your smartwatch as a viewfinder.
Rotate the Digital Crown to zoom.
- ❖ Touch the **White Shutter** to snap the picture

The pictures you take will be stored in the Photos application on your phone, but you can review them on your watch.

Record videos

- ❖ Enter the Camera Remote application 📷 on your smartwatch.
- ❖ Set up your phone to frame the shot using your smartwatch as a viewfinder.
Rotate the Digital Crown to zoom.
- ❖ Press & hold the Shutter button to start recording the video
- ❖ Release the Shutter button when you want to stop recording

Review your shots

Adhere to the directives below to review your shots on your smartwatch.

❖ View a picture: Touch the thumbnail in the lower-left corner of your display.
❖ See more pictures: Swipe to the right or left.
❖ Rotate the Digital Crown to zoom.
❖ Double-tap a picture to make it fill the screen
❖ Hide or display the shot count & the Close button: Touch your watch display.

Switch the camera & change settings

❖ Enter the Camera Remote application on your smartwatch.
❖ Click on the More Options icon ••• ., and then choose from the following options:
  ➢ Timer (Activate or deactivate the 3-seconds timer)
  ➢ Camera (back or front)
  ➢ Flash (off, on, or auto)
  ➢ Live Photo (off, on, or auto)

COMPASS

The Compass application  displays your watch's location, elevation, and the direction it is facing. You can save your location as a waypoint and then view the distance & direction to any waypoint you've created.

Select the type of compass

There are 5 different views in the Compass application.

❖ When you launch the Compass application for the first time, you'll see your bearing in the middle of the watch face.

❖ Rotate the Digital Crown down to show a big compass arrow with your watch's heading under the arrow.

❖ Rotate the Digital Crown up 2 screens to view your coordinates, elevation, & incline in the compass inner ring. You will see your current bearing in the outer ring. Nearby waypoints are displayed in the middle.

❖ Keep rotating the Digital Crown to see the location of the waypoints you've created and the waypoints that were automatically created to mark where you parked your vehicle, and give an estimate of the last place your smartwatch or phone could establish a mobile connection and where Emergency SOS was last available.

❖ Each screen that displays the compass dial has an Elevation button in the lower part of the screen. Click on the Elevation icon to see a

3D view of the waypoint elevation based on your current elevation.

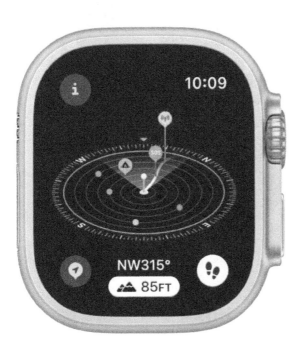

View compass details

In the Compass application, touch the Info icon in the upper left part of your display to see your coordinates (longitude & latitude), elevation, incline, & bearing.

Browse waypoints

You can view the waypoints that you have created

- ❖ Launch the Compass application
- ❖ Touch the Info icon ⓘ, and then click on the **Waypoints** button.
- ❖ Click on the **Compass Waypoints** button to see the waypoints you have created and the waypoints that were automatically created to mark where you parked your vehicle, and give an estimate of the last place your smartwatch

or phone could establish a mobile connection and where Emergency SOS was last available.

Add a bearing

❖ Launch the Compass application
❖ Touch the Info icon 🛈, and then click on the **Bearing** button.
❖ Rotate the Digital Crown to the bearing, and then click on the Mark icon ✅

To change the bearing, touch the Info icon,
scroll down, click on the **Bearing** button,
rotate the Digital Crown to another bearing,
and then touch the Mark icon .

❖ To delete the bearing, click on the Info icon ,
scroll down, and then click on the **Clear
Bearing** button.

Set a target elevation alert

If you set a target elevation, your Apple Watch
will notify you when you exceed the target so that
you can rest & acclimate as you go.

❖ Launch the Compass application.
❖ Click on the Info icon 🛈 , and click on the **Set Target Alert** button.
❖ Rotate the Digital Crown to choose the target elevation.

  To change the target, click the Info icon 🛈 , click on the **Target Alert** button, and select a new target level. To clear the target, click on the Info icon 🛈 , and then click on the **Clear Target** button.

Your watch will notify you when your target elevation is exceeded.

Use true north

Adhere to the directives below to use true north instead of magnetic north:

❖ Navigate to the Settings application.
❖ Click on the **Compass** button, and then activate **Use True North**.

If a red spinning radar screen appears

If your watch shows a red spinning radar screen when you enter the Compass app, it could be due to any of the below:

❖ Your watch might be in a poor magnetic environment: The compass may be affected by magnetic materials in your watch's band.
❖ Compass Calibration is deactivated: To enable or disable the **Compass Calibration** feature, simply navigate to the Setting application on your phone, touch Privacy & Security, touch Location Services, and then touch Systems Setting.
❖ Location Services is disabled: To enable or disable Location Services, simply navigate to the Settings application, click on the **Privacy** button, and then click on Location Services.

View & add Waypoints

Create & show Compass Waypoints

You can save your location as a waypoint and then view the distance & direction to any waypoint you've created.

❖ Navigate to the Compass application
❖ Click on the Waypoint icon🧭 to add a waypoint.
❖ Fill in the waypoint info such as symbol (work, or restaurant, for instance), colour, or name, and then click on the Add icon✅ .
❖ To view a Compass Waypoint, click on a waypoint on one of the 3 compass screens, rotate the Digital Crown to select a waypoint, and then touch the **Select** button.
Your watch screen will show the waypoint's distance, direction, & elevation—for instance, "4.5 miles to the left, down 356 ft."
❖ Click on the Edit icon✏️ to change the details of a selected waypoint and display the waypoint with its coordinates on the map.

Target a waypoint

You can target a waypoint to see its elevation, direction, & distance.

❖ Launch the Compass application.

❖ Click on the Info icon 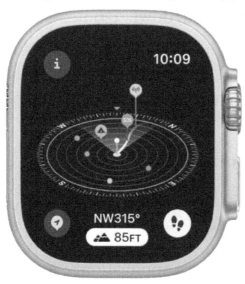, click on the **Waypoints** button, click Compass Waypoints or one of the guides, and then touch one of the waypoints

❖ Scroll down, and then click on the **Target Waypoint** button

Your screen will display the elevation, direction, & distance of the waypoint.

Use the Elevation dial

You can see waypoint elevations relative to your elevation.

❖ Navigate to the Compass application.

❖ On a compass screen, click on the Elevation icon in the lower part of your screen.

Waypoints that are in your smartwatch's direction are displayed with a column showing the elevations relative to your location. Waypoints that have Short columns are at lower elevations. A higher column indicates a higher elevation.

Drop a Compass Waypoint with the Action button

You can quickly drop a Compass Waypoint by pressing the Action button on your smartwatch.

❖ Navigate to the Settings application.
❖ Touch **Action button**, click on the **Action** button, click the **Waypoint** button, and then click the Back icon to go back to the actions list.
❖ Press the Action button on your smartwatch to drop a Custom Waypoint & display the edit screen.

Use the Backtrack feature to retrace your steps

Retrace your steps

With the Backtrack feature, you can track your path and then retrace your steps if you get lost.

❖ Launch the Compass application.

❖ Click the Backtrack icon 🔘, and then click on the **Start** button to start recording your route.

❖ To retrace your steps, touch the Pause icon ⏸ and then touch the **Retrace Steps** button. You will see where you first touched the Backtrack button 🔘 on the compass.

❖ Follow the path to go back to where you activated **Backtrack**.

❖ When you are done, click on the Back-track button 🔘, and then click on **Delete Steps**.

Start Backtrack with the Action button

❖ Navigate to the Settings application.

❖ Touch **Action button**, click on the **Action** button, click on the **Backtrack** button, and then click the Back icon 🔘 to go back to the actions list.

❖ Press the Actions button on your smartwatch to activate Backtrack

Press the Action button & the Side button simultaneously to pause the backtrack feature.

CYCLE TRACKING

You can record details of your menstrual cycle in the Cycle Tracking application . You can add flow data & symptoms like cramps, headaches, etc. Using the info you have recorded, the Cycle Tracking application can notify you when it predicts that your next fertile window or period is about to begin. If you wear your smartwatch to bed every night, the application can make use of your wrist temperature to make period prediction better and also give you a prediction of your next ovulation.

Setup Cycle Tracking

❖ Launch the Health application on your phone.
❖ Click on the **Browse** button to see the Health Categories screen
❖ Click on the **Cycle Tracking** button
❖ Click on **Get Started**, and then adhere to the directives on your display to set notifications & other options.

To remove or add options after you've setup Cycle Tracking, simply launch the Health application on your phone, click on the **Browse** button, click on Cycle Tracking, and then click on Options beside Cycle Log.

Record your cycle on your watch

❖ Launch the Cycle Tracking application.
❖ Carry out any of the below:
  ➢ Record a period on a specific day: With the date displayed on the timeline, touch the **Log** button. Touch the **Period** button, select a flow rate, and then touch the Done button .
  ➢ Record symptoms, & other info: With the date displayed on the timeline, touch **Log**. Click on any of the categories, pick one of the options, and then touch the Done button .

The observations you record will be displayed in the cycle log on your phone. If you have enabled Fertility Notifications & Period Notifications in the Health application on your phone, you'll get notifications on your watch about retrospectives ovulation estimates, fertility window prediction, & upcoming periods.

You can also record factors that may affect your cycle (like breastfeeding, pregnancy, & birth control) in the Health application on your iPhone. Depending on the factors you pick, retrospective ovulation estimates, fertility window forecast, & your period forecast may be disabled on your smartwatch & phone.

Get retrospective ovulation estimates

When worn to bed every night, your watch can track your temperature change while you sleep & use this info to provide retrospective ovulation estimate & make period prediction better.

Setup wrist temperature tracking

- ❖ Setup Sleep monitoring(in the Sleep application) and Cycle Tracking
- ❖ To determine your temperature, make sure the Sleep Focus is turned on, and then wear your watch while you sleep.
  The Wrist temperature information will be available after 5 nights.
- ❖ To check the temperature info, navigate to the Health application on your phone, click on the **Browse** button in the lower part of your display, click on **Body Measurement**, and then click on **Wrist Temperature**.

You should be able to see your retrospective ovulation prediction after 2 menstrual cycles of putting on your watch to bed every night.

Disable Wrist Temperature for Cycle Tracking

- ❖ Enter the Health application on your phone, click on the **Browse** button, and then click on the **Cycle Tracking** button.
- ❖ Scroll down, click on **Options**, and then disable the **Use Wrist Temperature** feature.

If you deactivate wrist temperature monitoring, you will not receive retrospective ovulation estimates anymore and your wrist temperature will not be used to predict your period.

DEPTH

You can use the Depth application on your smartwatch to measure water temperature, depth to 130ft, & underwater duration.

WARNING: Underwater activity is hazardous. If you're making use of the Apple Watch in a situation where failure of the device could result in environmental damage, injury, or death, always make use of a secondary depth sensor & watch/timer.

Depth application overview

The Depth application provides basic info that is easy to check during recreational underwater activities like shallow free-diving, pool swims, snorkeling, etc.

Please note: The Depth application isn't a substitute for a dive computer.

Your smartwatch will display the following on one screen:

- ❖ Present time
- ❖ Your depth & maximum depth
- ❖ How long you have been underwater
- ❖ The temperature of the water

Setup the Depth application

When setting up your smartwatch, you choose how you want the Depth application to open— automatically when your watch is submerged, or manually, when you touch the application icon or press the Actions button. To change the setting, simply adhere to the directives below:

❖ Enter the Settings application on your smartwatch.
❖ Touch General, and then touch Auto-Launch
❖ Activate or deactivate Auto-Launch App in the **When Submerged** section

Or, enter the Watch application on your phone, touch the **My Watch** button, head over to General> Auto-Launch, then activate or deactivate Auto-Launch App in the **When Submerged** section

❖ To pick temperature & depth units, touch the **Depth** button in the Settings application, and then pick water temperature units (Celsius or Fahrenheit) & depth units (Meters or Feet).

You can also launch the Watch application on your phone, touch the **My Watch** button, and then click on the **Depth** button.

Start & end your dive

The Depth application activates when your smartwatch is submerged in water. When you submerge your watch in water, the screen will lock and the Water Lock will activate.

Once you come out of the water, long-press the Digital Crown to deactivate the Water Lock feature, which removes water from the speaker.

View your dive history

❖ Launch the Depth application on your smartwatch
❖ Click on the **View Recent Dives** button
   Recent dives will appear, showing when the dive started, the maximum depth of the dive, and how long you spent underwater
❖ Touch a dive to view more details

ECG

An ECG (also known as EKG or electrocardiogram) is a test that helps to record the intensity & timing of the electrical signals that make your heart beat. By observing an ECG, a doctor can gain a deep understanding of a heart rhythm & check for abnormalities.

The Apple Watch has an electrical heart-sensor that allows you to take an ECG.

The ECG application isn't designed for individuals below the age of 22.

Install & setup the ECG application

The ECG application is installed on your smartwatch when you set it up in the Health application on your iPhone. Follow the directives below to setup the ECG application:

❖ Launch the Health application on your phone.
❖ Adhere to the directives on your screen. If the screen does not show any prompt to setup ECG, simply click on the **Browse** button in

the lower part of your screen, click on **Heart**, touch Electrocardiogram (ECG), and then click on Setup ECG App.

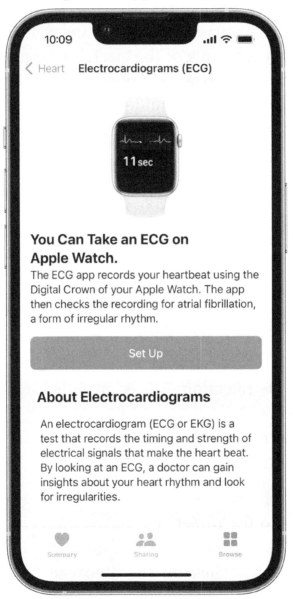

❖ After completing the setup, launch the ECG application ᪲ on your smartwatch to take an ECG test.

If you still do not see the ECG application on your smartwatch, enter the Watch application on your phone and touch the **Heart** button. Under ECG, touch the **Install** button to install the ECG application.

Take an ECG

❖ Make sure your smartwatch isn't too loose or tight & it is on the wrist you selected in the Watch application. To check, enter the Watch application on your phone, click on the **My Watch** button, and then head over to General>Watch Orientation.

❖ Enter the ECG application ᪲ on your smartwatch

❖ Put your hand on your lap or a table

❖ Use one of your fingers to hold the Digital Crown. You do not have to press your watch's Digital Crown while the test is going on

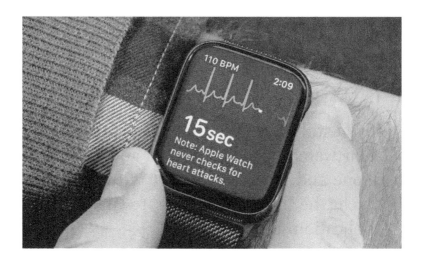

❖ Wait. The test will take around Thirty seconds. After the session, you'll be sent a classification, then you can click on the **Add Symptoms** button and pick your symptoms.

❖ Touch **Save** to store any symptoms, and then click on the **Done** button.

How to read the results

After a session, you'll be sent one of the following results in the ECG application. Regardless of what the result states, if you're not feeling well you should see a doctor.

Inconclusive

When the result is inconclusive, it means the recording cannot be classified.

AFib

An Atrial fibrillation result means your heart is beating abnormally. Atrial fibrillation is a very common form of heart palpitations or arrhythmia.

Sinus rhythm

It means that your heart beats in a uniform pattern between 50 & 100BPM.

High or low heart rate

In ECG version 1, a heartrate that's below 50BPM or above 120BPM can affect the application's ability to check for Atrial Fibrillation. A heartrate that's under 50BPM or above 150BPM in ECG version 2 can affect the application's ability to check for Atrial Fibrillation

❖ A heartrate can be high as a result of stress, Atrial fibrillation, infection, dehydration, exercise, alcohol, or other arrhythmias.

❖ A heartrate could be low because of some medications or electric signals aren't conducted through the heart properly.

View & share your health info

The ECG Wave form, its related classifications, and any noted symptoms will be stored in the Health application on your iPad or iPhone. You can also share the data as a PDF file with your doctor.

❖ Launch the Health application on your phone.
❖ On your iPhone, touch the **Browse** button. On your iPad, touch the Sidebar icon 🔲 to reveal the sidebar
❖ Click on the **Heart** button, and then touch the **Electrocardiogram (ECG)** button.
❖ Touch the chart to check your ECG results.
❖ Touch the **Export PDF for your Doctor** option.

❖ Click on the Share button ⬆️ to share or print the file.

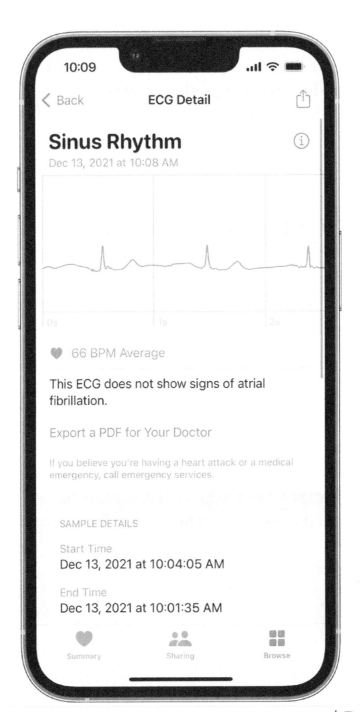

FIND PEOPLE

You can use the Find People application  to know the location of people you care about & also share your location with these people. If the individual has an Apple Watch Ultra, iPad, or iPhone, and shares their location with you, you will be able to see the person's location on a map. You can set your smartwatch to notify you when someone leaves or arrives at a location.

Add a friend

❖ Enter the Find People application  .
❖ Touch the **Share My Location** button.

❖ Click on the Keypad, Contacts, or Dictation button to pick a friend
❖ Choose a phone number or e-mail address
❖ Choose the duration— you can decide to share your location indefinitely, for an hour, or till the end of that day.

Your friend will be informed that you have shared your location with them. They may also decide to share their location with you. After your friend has agreed to share their location with you, you'll be able to see their location in a list or a map in the Find People application on your watch or in the Find My application on your MacOS device, iPad, & iPhone.

If you want to stop sharing your location with someone, touch the name of the friend in the Find People screen, and then click on the **Stop Sharing** button.

If you want to stop sharing your location with everybody, simply navigate to the Settings application on your smartwatch, touch Privacy & Security, click on Location Services, and then disable the **Share My Location** feature.

Find your friends' locations

❖ Launch the Find People application to see your friends list, with the location & distance of each friend from you. Roll the Digital Crown to see more people.
❖ Click on any of your friends in the list to see where they are on a map & their address.

Return to friends list.

Scroll to get directions or send a message.

❖ Touch the Back icon to go back to the friends list.

Notify your friend of your arrival or departure

❖ Launch the Find People application on your smartwatch.
❖ Click on one of your friends from the list, scroll down, and then click on **Notify [friend's name]**.
❖ Enable **Notify [friend's name]** on the next screen, and then choose to notify the

individual when you leave where you are or get to their location.

Receive an alert about your friend's location

❖ Navigate to the Find People application on your smartwatch.
❖ Click on a friend from the list, scroll down, and then click on the **Notify Me** button.
❖ Activate **Notify Me**, and then choose to receive a notification when your friend leaves where they are or reaches your location.

Receive directions to a friend

❖ Launch the Find People application on your smartwatch.
❖ Click on a friend in the list, scroll down, and then click on the **Directions** button to launch the Maps application.
❖ Click on the route to receive directions from where you are to the current location of your friend.

Contact a friend

❖ Launch the Find People application on your smartwatch.
❖ Click on a friend in the list, scroll down, click on **Contacts**, and then touch a number or e-mail address.

FIND DEVICES & ITEMS

You can use the Find Device application on your smartwatch to find your misplaced Apple devices.

Enable the Find My network for your smartwatch

If your smartwatch is paired with your phone, the **Find My network** is automatically setup when you activate the **Find My iPhone** feature. With the Find My network feature activated, you will be able to find your watch even when it is switched off or disconnected.

- ❖ Navigate to the Settings application on your watch.
- ❖ Touch your name, and scroll down till you find your smartwatch.
- ❖ Click on your watch's name, and then click on the **Find My Watch** button.
- ❖ Enable the **Find My network** feature if it is not on.

See a device's location

If your device is online, you can find its location in the Find Device application. For some devices, the Find Device application can find the device even when it is in Low Power Mode, switched off, or if Airplane Mode is enabled.

Launch the Find Device application on your watch, and then click on any of the devices.

❖ If the device cannot be found: You will see **"No Location"** under the name of the device. Under Notifications, enable **Notify When Found**. You'll be notified once the location becomes available.
❖ If the device can be found: You will see its location on the map. The approximate distance to the device, when last it was connected to a mobile or WiFi network, & its charge level will appear at the top of the map.

Play a sound on your watch, Mac, iPad, or iPhone

❖ Launch the Find Device application on your smartwatch, and then touch the device you would like to play a sound on.

❖ Touch the **Play Sound** button.
  ➤ If the device is online: The sound will start playing and it will play for the next 2 minutes. A "Find My Device" notification will appear on the screen of the device.
  A confirmation e-mail will also be sent to your Apple e-mail address
  ➤ If the device is not online: Your screen will display a **Sound Pending** alert. The sound will play the next time the device connects to a mobile or WiFi network.

Play sound on your Beats headphones or AirPods

If your Beats headphone or AirPod is connected to your watch, you can play a sound on them.

❖ Launch the Find Devices application, and then click on a device on the list.
❖ Touch the **Play Sound** button.
  ➤ If the device is online: The sound will start playing and it will play for the next 2 minutes.
  A confirmation e-mail will also be sent to your Apple e-mail address

➢ If the device is not online: You'll be notified the next time the device is in range of your smartwatch.

Receive directions to a device

❖ Launch the Find Devices application , and then click on the device you'd like to receive directions to.
❖ Click on **Directions** to launch he Maps application.
❖ Touch the route to receive directions from where you are to the location of the device.

Be notified when you leave a device behind

You can get notifications when you leave your device behind so you don't misplace it. You can also setup Trusted Places - places where you can leave your device without being notified.

❖ Launch the Find Device application

❖ Touch the device you'd like to setup a notification for.
❖ Under Notifications, click on the **Notify When Left Behind** button, and then enable **Notify When Left Behind**.

Or, enter the Find My application on your phone, click on **Devices**, click on the device you'd like to set a notification for, and then click on **Notify When Left Behind**. Enable **Notify When Left Behind**, and then adhere to the guidelines on the screen.

To add a Trusted Location, just choose one of the suggested locations, or click on **New Location**, choose a location on the map, and then click on **Done**.

Mark a device as lost

If you lost your device, you can enable Lost Mode or lock your Mac.

❖ Launch the Find Devices application on your smartwatch, and then touch the device

❖ Touch the Lost Mode button, and then enable the Lost Mode feature.

Here's what happens when a device is marked as lost:

❖ Apple Pay will be deactivated on the device
❖ You will see the location of the device on the map.
❖ A confirmation e-mail will be sent to your Apple ID e-mail address.
❖ A message will appear on the device's lock screen stating that the device is lost and how to reach you.
❖ The device will not show alerts or make noise when it receives notifications

Locate an AirTag or other items

You can find a missing AirTag or 3rd-party item that you've registered to your Apple ID.

See an item's location

Launch the Find Items application on your watch, and then click on one of the devices.

❖ If the item cannot be found: You'll see when & where it was last located. Under Notifications, touch the **Notify When Found** button, and then enable **Notify When Found**. You'll be notified once the location becomes available.
❖ If the item can be found: You will see its location on the map. The approximate distance to the device, when last it was connected to a mobile or WiFi network, & its charge level will appear at the top of the map.

Play a sound

If the item is close by, you can play a sound on it to make it easier to find the item.

❖ Launch the Find Items application, and then click on the item you'd like to play a sound on.
❖ Touch the **Play Sound** button.
Click on **Stop Sound** to stop playing the sound before it stops by itself.

Receive directions to an item

You can receive directions to the present or last known location of an item in the Maps application on your smartwatch.

* Navigate to the Find Items application, and then touch the item you'd like to receive directions to.
* Click on the **Directions** button to enter the Maps application.
* Touch the route to receive directions to the location of the item.

Be notified when you leave an item behind

You can get notifications when you leave an item behind so you don't misplace it. You can also setup Trusted Places - places where you can leave your item without being notified.

* Launch the Find Items application on your smartwatch, and then touch the item you'd like to setup a notification for.
* Click on the **Notify When Left Behind** button, and then enable the **Notify When Left Behind** feature.

Or, launch the Find My application on your phone, click on the **Items** button, click on the item you'd like to set a notification for, and then click on **Notify When Left Behind**. Enable **Notify When Left Behind**, and then adhere to the guidelines on the screen.

To add a Trusted Location, just choose one of the suggested locations, or click on **New Location**, choose a location on the map, and then click on **Done**.

Mark a device as lost

If your AirTag or a 3rd-party item registered to your Apple ID is stolen or misplaced, you can enable Lost Mode.

❖ Launch the Find Items application ⊕, and then click on the item
❖ Touch the Lost Mode button, and then enable the Lost Mode feature.

If someone finds the missing item, they can get more info about the item when they connect to it.

Disable Lost Mode

Deactivate Lost Mode when you find the item you misplaced

❖ Launch the Find Items application ⊞, and then click on the item
❖ Touch the Lost Mode button, and then disable the Lost Mode feature.

HEART

The heart rate is a great way to monitor the body's health.

Check your heart rate

Launch the Heart Rate application on your smartwatch to see your heart rate, walking average rate, & resting rate.

Your watch will continue to measure your heartrate as long as you are putting it on.

View your heart rate data graph

❖ Launch the Heart Rate application on your smartwatch.
❖ Roll the Digital Crown to Walking Average, Resting, & current Heart rate to see your heart rate for the day.

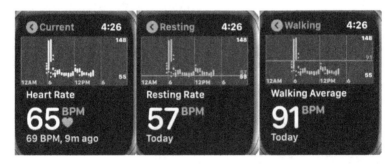

To view more heart rate data, launch the Health application on your iPhone, click on the **Browse** button, click on the **Heart** button, and then click on an entry. You can view heartrate for the past year, month, week, day, or hour.

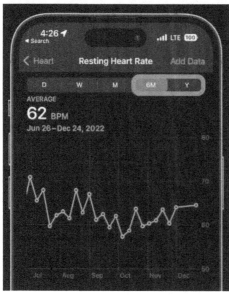

Activate heart rate data

❖ Navigate to the Settings application
❖ Head over to Privacy and Security, and then touch Health
❖ Click on the **Heart Rate** button, and then activate the **Heart Rate** feature

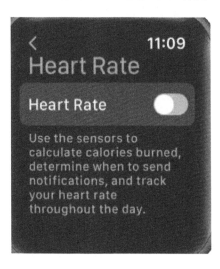

Get low or high heart rate alerts

❖ Navigate to the Settings application, and then click on the **Heart** button
❖ Click on Low Rate Notification or High Heart Rate Notification, and then select a heart rate limit.

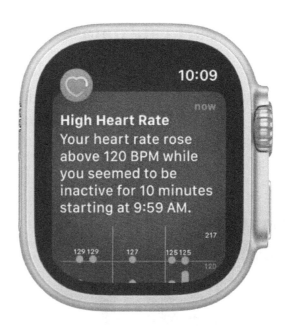

Or launch the Watch application on your smartphone, click on the **My Watch** button, and then click on the **Heart** button. Click on Low Heart-Rate or High Heart-Rate, and then select a limit.

Setup irregular heart rate alert

Your smartwatch will notify you if it detects an irregular heart rhythm like AFib.

❖ Launch the Watch application on your smartphone
❖ Click on the **My Watch** tab, click on the **Heart** button, and then click on setup Irregular Rhythm Notification in Health
❖ In the Health application, click on Setup, and then adhere to the directives on your display.

MEMOJI

You can create your own Memoji in the Memoji application.

Create a Memoji

- ❖ Navigate to the Memoji application on your smartwatch.
- ❖ If this is the first time you are using the Memoji application, click on the **Get Started** button.

If you have created a Memoji before, scroll up, and then click on the Add Memoji icon  to add another one.

❖ Click on each feature and rotate the Digital Crown to select your preferred Memoji options.

❖ Click on the Done icon to add it to your Memoji collection.

To create another Memoji, click on the Add Memoji icon , and add features.

Edit Memoji & more

Launch the Memoji application, click on a Memoji, and then select one of the options:

- ❖ Edit a Memoji: select features like headwear, and then roll the Digital Crown to select one of the variations.
- ❖ Create a Memoji watch face: Scroll down, and then click on the **Create Watch Face** button. Go back to the watch face and swipe left continuously till you get to the Memoji watch face.
- ❖ Duplicate a Memoji: click on the **Duplicate** button.
- ❖ Delete a Memoji: Click on the **Delete** button.

MUSIC

When you add songs to your smartwatch, you can listen to them at any time, even when your iPhone is not with you.

Add music using your iPhone

❖ Launch the Watch application on your phone.
❖ Click on the **My Watch** button, and then click on **Music**

❖ In the Playlists & Albums section, click on the **Add Music** button.

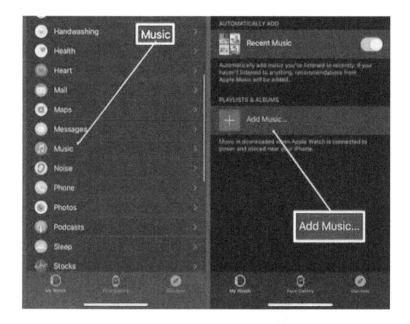

❖ Choose playlists and albums you would like to synchronize to your watch, and then click on the Add icon ⊕ to add them to the Playlist and Albums queue.

Music will be added when your smartwatch is placed close to your iPhone.

Add music using the watch

If you are an Apple Music subscriber, you can add music with your smartwatch.

❖ Launch the Music application .

❖ In the Listen Now screen, go to the song you would like to add
Or, from the Listen Now screen, click on the Back button ◀, touch **Search**, and then look for the song you want to add.

❖ Click on an album or playlist, click the More Options icon ⚫⚫⚫, and then touch the **Add to Library** button.
An alert will appear confirming that the item has been added.
Note: You can stream the songs you've added to your smartwatch when you are connected to

the Internet. If you want to play a song offline, you'll need to download it first.

❖ To download the song to your smartwatch, touch the More Options button once more, and then touch the **Download** button.

Add a workout playlist

You can add a playlist that will automatically start playing when you begin a workout in the Workout application on your watch.

❖ Enter the Watch application on your phone.
❖ Touch the **My Watch** tab, and then click on the **Workout** button.
❖ Click on the **Workout Playlists** button, and then pick one of the playlists.

The playlists will be added to My Watch> Music in the Apple Watch application on your smartphone.

Please note: The workout playlist will not start playing if you are currently listening to other songs.

Remove songs from your smartwatch

Note: To check the amount of songs saved on your watch, simply enter the Settings application on your watch, touch General, and then touch Storage.

Remove music using phone

❖ Navigate to the Watch application on your smartphone.
❖ Touch the **My Watch** button, click on Music, and then carry out any of the below:
  ➢ For the songs you have added: Touch the **Edit** button, and then touch the Delete icon ⊖ beside the item you'd like to remove.
  ➢ For songs that were automatically added: Disable **Recent Music** or other songs automatically added to your smartwatch.

Songs you delete from your watch will remain on your phone.

Remove music using your smartwatch

If you are an Apple Music subscriber, you can remove songs directly on your smartwatch.

❖ Enter the Music application 🎵 on your smartwatch
❖ From the Listen Now screen, click on the Back button ◀, click on the **Library** button, scroll down, click on the **Downloaded** button, and then click Albums or Playlist.
❖ Choose one of the playlists or albums, click on the More Options icon •••, and then touch the **Remove** button.
❖ Choose the Remove Downloads or Delete from Library option.

Note: You can also delete individual songs. To do this, just swipe a song to the left, touch the More Options button •••, touch Delete from Library, and then click on the **Delete** button.

Play music on your watch

After connecting your watch to a Bluetooth speaker or headphone, enter the Music application, and then carry out any of the below:

Tap for more options.

❖ Play songs on your smartwatch: Rotate the Digital Crown to go through the Listen Now screen, and then click on one of the categories, playlists, or albums.

❖ Play songs from your music library: From the Listen Now screen, click on the Back button touch the **Library** button, touch one of the categories like Downloaded, Album, or Playlists, and then select music.

❖ Search the Apple Music Library: Touch the **Search** button, enter a song, artist, or album, and then click on the **Search** button. Touch one of the results to play it.

MEASURE NOISE LEVELS

The Noise application  on your smartwatch measures the sound level in your surroundings. When your smartwatch detects that the decibel level has gotten to a point that could affect your ear, it can alert you with a tap on your wrist.

Setup the Noise application

❖ Enter the Noise application on your smartwatch.

- ❖ Touch the **Enable** button to activate monitoring.
- ❖ In the future, simply enter the Noise application to measure the noise in your environment.

Receive noise notifications

- ❖ Navigate to the Settings application.
- ❖ Touch Noise> Noise Notification, and then pick any of the settings.

Or, launch the Watch application on your phone, click on the **My Watch** button, head over to Noise> Noise Threshold

Deactivate noise measuring

- ❖ Launch the Settings application.
- ❖ Head over to Noise> Environmental Sound Measurement, and then deactivate **Measure Sounds**.

View noise notification details

You can receive an alert on your iPhone from your watch when the noise around you gets to a point that could affect your ear.

To see the details of an alert, adhere to the guidelines below:

❖ Launch the Health application on your smartphone, and then click on the **Summary** tab in the lower part of the screen.
❖ Touch the notification close to the upper part of your display, and then touch the **Show More Data** button.

VOICE MEMOS

You can record personal notes with the Voice Memos application.

Record a voice memo

❖ Launch the Voice Memos application on your smartwatch.
❖ Touch the Record button ●.
❖ Touch the Stop Recording button ● to stop recording.

Play a voice memo

* Launch the Voice Memos application 🔵 on your smartwatch
* Choose any of the recordings on the voice Memo screen, and then click on the Play icon 🔵 to play the voice Memo.
* To move forward or skip back, click the Skip Ahead icon ⓑ or Skip Back icon ⓑ .
* To rename or delete the recording, simply touch the More Options button 🔵, and then select one of the options.

SLEEP

You can create a sleep schedule in the Sleep application to help you reach your sleep goals. Wear your smartwatch to bed, and it can track how much time you spend in each stage of sleep—Deep, Core, & REM—as well as when you wake up. When you wake up, enter the Sleep application to see how much sleep you've had & what your sleep patterns have been over the last fourteen days.

You can setup more than one sleep schedule, for instance, one schedule for weekends & another one for weekdays.

Setup sleep on your smartwatch

❖ Navigate to the Sleep application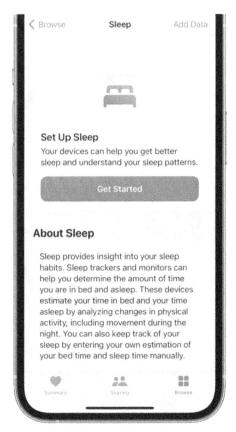 on your smartwatch.

❖ Adhere to the directives on the screen.

Or, launch the Health application on your smartphone, touch the **Browse** tab, click on the **Sleep** button, and then click on the **Get Started** button in the Setup Sleep section.

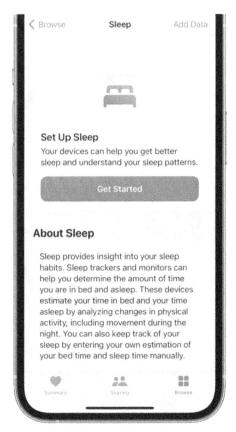

Change or turn off the next wakeup alarm

❖ Navigate to the Sleep application on your smartwatch.
❖ Click on the Wake up Alarm icon .
❖ To set a new wakeup time, click on the wakeup time, roll the Digital Crown to select a new time, and then touch .

Deactivate **Alarm** if you do not want your smartwatch to wake you up in the morning.

This change only applies to your next wakeup alarm, after which your normal routine will resume.

Change or add a sleep schedule

❖ Enter the Sleep application⊖ on your smartwatch.

❖ Click on the Alarm icon ⏰ .

❖ Roll the Digital Crown scroll to Full Schedule, and then do any of the below:
  ➢ Touch the current sleep schedule to change it
  ➢ Touch the **Add Schedule** button to add a sleep schedule.
  ➢ Change your sleep target: Click on **Sleep Goals**, then set your sleep duration
  ➢ Make changes to wind-down time: Click on **Wind Down**, and then set how long you want the Sleep Focus to be active before your bed time.

❖ Carry out any of the below:
  ➢ Set your schedule days: Touch your schedule, and then click on the **Active On** button. Select days, and then touch ◀ .
  ➢ Change your bedtime & wakeup time: Touch your schedule, touch the Wakeup button or the Bedtime button, rotate the Digital Crown to select a new time, and then click on ✓ .

➢ Set alarm options: Click on your schedule, then disable or enable Alarm and touch Sounds & Haptic to select an alarm sound.
➢ Delete or cancel a schedule: Click on your schedule, and then click on the **Delete Schedule** button to remove a schedule, or click on the **Cancel** icon⊗ to cancel creating a new schedule.

Check out your sleep history

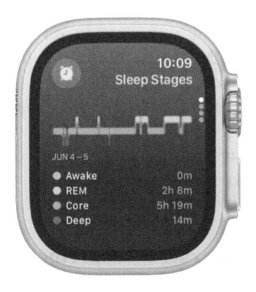

Launch the Sleep application⊖ on your smartwatch to check how much sleep you had in the previous night, how long you spent in the different sleep stages & your sleep average over the past fourteen days.

Check your sleep respiratory rate

Your smartwatch can monitor your breathing rate while you sleep, which can give you more information about your health. After wearing your smartwatch to bed, adhere to the guidelines below:

❖ Navigate to the Health application on your phone, touch the **Browse** button, and then click on **Respiratory**.
❖ Click on Respiratory Rate, and then touch **Show Respiratory Rate Data**.
The sleep entry will show the range of your respiratory rate when you were asleep.

Disable respiratory rate measurements

❖ Head over to the Settings application
❖ Touch Privacy and Security> Health

❖ Click on the **Respiratory Rate** button, and then disable Respiratory Rate.

Monitor your nightly wrist temperature

When worn to bed, your smartwatch can monitor your wrist temperature changes every night to give you more information about your health.

Setup wrist temperature tracking

❖ Turn on Track Sleep with Apple Watch (in the Sleep application)
Or, enter the Watch application on your smartphone, click on the **My Watch** button, click on **Sleep**, and then touch **Track Sleep with Apple Watch** to activate this feature.
❖ To set a temperature baseline, make sure Sleep Focus is enabled, and then wear your smartwatch while you sleep.
Wrist temperature info will become available after 5 nights.

Review your wrist temperature

- ❖ Enter the Health application on your smartphone, then touch the **Browse** tab
- ❖ Touch Body Measurement, and then touch Wrist Temperature
- ❖ Touch a point in the chart to see sample details

Disable wrist temperature tracking

- ❖ Navigate to the Settings application on your smartwatch
- ❖ Touch Privacy and Security> Health
- ❖ Click on the **Wrist Temperature** button, and then disable Wrist Temperature.

Or, navigate to the Watch application on your smartphone, click on the My Watch button, click on the Privacy button, and then deactivate wrist Temperature.

APPLE PAY

You can use Apple Pay to pay for items.

Add a card to your smartwatch with your phone

- ❖ Launch the Watch application on your phone.
- ❖ Click on the **My Watch** button, and then click on Wallet and Apple Pay.
- ❖ If you have a card on another Apple device or a card you've recently removed, click on the **Add** button beside the card you want to add, and then type the CVV of the card.
- ❖ For other cards, click on the **Add Card** button and then adhere to the directives on your screen.

Your card provider may ask for more steps to verify your information.

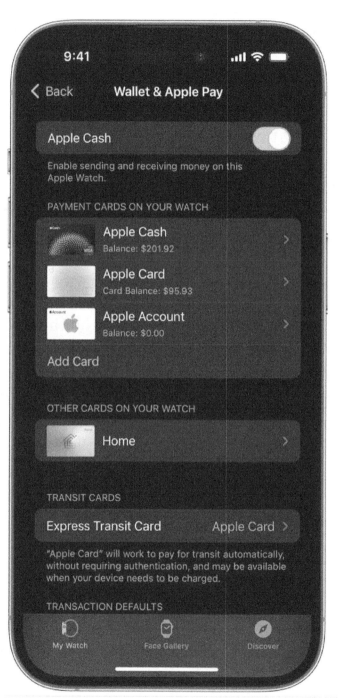

Add a card on your smartwatch

❖ Enter the Wallet application on your smartwatch.
❖ Click on the More Options icon ⦿ , and then click the **Add Card** button.
❖ Pick Apple Account, Transit Card, and Credit or Debit Card; and then adhere to the directives on your display.

Choose your default card

❖ Launch the Wallet application ⦿ on your smartwatch.
❖ Click on the More Options icon ⦿ , click on the **Default Card** button, and then choose one of the cards.

Or, launch the Watch application on your phone, touch the **My Watch** button, touch Wallet & Apple Pay, click on the **Default Card** button, and then pick one of the cards.

Remove the card from Apple Pay

❖ Launch the Wallet application on your smartwatch.
❖ Touch a card to select it
❖ Scroll down, and then click on the **Remove** button.

Or, enter the Watch application on your phone, click on the **My Watch** button, click on the **Wallet & Apple Pay** button, touch the card, and then click on the **Remove Card** button.

Pay for items in a store with your smartwatch

❖ Press the side button twice quickly.
❖ Scroll to select a card.
❖ Take your smartwatch very close to the contactless card reader, with the screen facing the reader.

You will feel a tap on your wrist and your watch will beep to confirm that the payment details have been sent. You'll be notified when the transaction is confirmed.

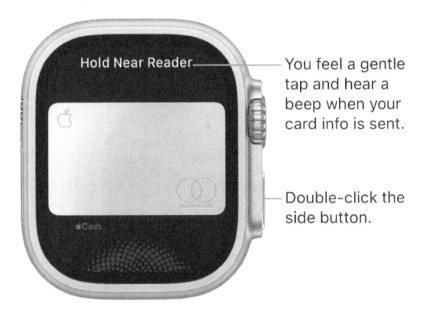

Hold Near Reader — You feel a gentle tap and hear a beep when your card info is sent.

Double-click the side button.

Make in-app purchases

❖ When purchasing items in an application on your watch, pick the **Apple Pay** option at checkout.

❖ Go through the billing, shipping, & payment info, and then press the side button twice quickly to make a payment with your smartwatch.

WORKOUT

The Workout application provides tools that can help you manage your workout sessions.

Start a workout

* Launch the Workout application.
* Rotate the Digital Crown to select one of the workouts.
  Click on the **Add Workout** button at the end of the screen to add workouts like surfing or kickboxing.

❖ When you are ready to start, touch the workout.

Tap to set workout goals.

Turn the Digital Crown to choose another workout.

Start a workout with the Action button

You can assign a favourite workout to the Action button.

❖ Launch the Settings application.
❖ Click on **Action Button**, click on **Action**, touch the **Workout** button, and then touch the Back icon to go back to the actions list.

- ❖ Click on the **First Press** button, click on Start a Workout, and then select one of the workouts
- ❖ When you want to start a workout, simply press the Action button
  Press the Action button & the Side button simultaneously to pause the workout.

Pause & resume a workout

To pause a workout, press the Digital Crown & the side button simultaneously. Or, swipe right on a workout screen, and then click on the **Pause** button. Click on the **Resume** button to resume the workout.

Start an outdoor push wheelchair workout

If you specified that you're a wheelchair user, you can begin an outdoor push workout in the Workout application. Your smartwatch will track your pushes instead of steps, and you are allowed to choose the pace too.

Set your wheelchair status in Health info

Adhere to the directives below to set your wheelchair status:

* Enter the Watch application on your phone.
* Click on the **My Watch** button, touch the **Health** button, and then click on Health Details.
* Click on the **Edit** button, click on the **Wheelchair** button, and then touch the **Yes** option.
* Touch the **Done** button

Start an outdoor push exercise

* Launch the Workout application.

❖ Rotate the Digital Crown to Outdoor Push Walking pace or Outdoor Push Running Pace.
❖ Touch the workout when you are ready to start.

Adjust your smartwatch during a workout

You can do any of the below while working out:

❖ Check your progress: Raise your hand to check your workout statistics, like your heart rate, the calories you've burned, etc. Rotate the Digital Crown to see other workout views.
❖ Rock out while working out: While working out, swipe left to the Now Play screen to pick songs and control the volume on your Bluetooth headphone. To pick a playlist that automatically starts playing when you start a workout, simply enter the Watch application on your phone, and then touch the **My Watch** button. Touch the **Workout** button, touch the **Workout Playlist** button, and then select one of the playlists.

Switch workout views while working out

Start a workout, and then rotate the Digital Crown to cycle through the workout view options.

Customize workout views

❖ Launch the Workout application.
❖ Roll the Digital Crown to one of the workouts

- ❖ Touch the More Options icon, scroll down, and then touch the **Preferences** button.
- ❖ Click on [name of workout] Workout Views.
- ❖ Scroll, and then touch **Include** beside the metrics you want.

Use gym equipment with your smartwatch

Your watch can pair & synchronize date with compatible gym equipment like indoor bikes, treadmills, etc., giving you more accurate workout info.

- ❖ Check if the device is compatible - you will see "Connect to Apple Watch" on the device.
- ❖ Ensure your smartwatch is set to detect gym equipment—launch the Setting application on your watch, touch the **Workout** button, and then enable **Detect Gym Equipment**.
- ❖ Take your smartwatch very close to the contactless reader of the gym device, with your watch screen facing the reader.
  You'll feel a tap and your watch will beep to confirm that it has connected
- ❖ Press the **Start** button on the gym equipment to start the workout. Press the **Stop** button to end the workout session.

If Detect Gym Equipment is disabled in the Settings application, enter the Workout application, and then take your watch very close to the contactless reader on the gym device, with your watch screen facing the reader.

End the workout

When you reach your target, you'll hear a sound & feel a vibration. If you feel fine and want to continue, you can—your smartwatch will continue to collect the data till you decide to stop. Adhere to the directives below to stop a workout:

❖ Swipe right on the workout screen, click on the **End** button, and then touch the **End Workout** button.

❖ Rotate the Digital Crown to view your workout summary, and then click on the **Done** button at the end of the summary.

Review your workout history

❖ Launch the Fitness application on your phone.

❖ Click on the **Show More** button beside
History, and then touch one of the workouts.

Change your workout goals

You can modify existing workouts to create the one you want.

❖ Launch the Workout application.
❖ Rotate the Digital Crown to one of the workouts.
❖ Click the More options icon⬤, and then click on the **Create Workout** button.
❖ Touch a goal like Time or Calorie; select a value, and then click on the **Done** button
❖ Click on the modified goal to start the workout.

Or, click on the Back icon 🔘 to save the edited workout, and then click the workout when you are ready to start.

To remove an edited goal from a workout, go to the workout, click on the More Options icon 🔘, click on the Edit icon 🔘 beside the edited goal, scroll down, click on the **Delete Workout** button, and then click on the **Delete** button.

Combine several activities into one workout

- ❖ Launch the Workout application.
- ❖ Start the first workout.
- ❖ When you are ready to begin another exercise, simply swipe right, click on the **End** button, touch the **New Workout** button, and then pick a workout.
- ❖ When you're done with all the activities, swipe right, touch the **End** button, and then click on the **End Workout** button.
- ❖ Roll the Digital Crown to go through the workout result summary.

❖ Scroll down and touch the **Done** button to save the workout

Create a Multisport workout

You can combine swimming, cycling, & running workouts in a Multisport workout, and your smartwatch will automatically recognize when you switch between them.

❖ Launch the Workout application.
❖ Carry out any of the below:
  ➤ If this is the first time you are creating a multisport workout: Click on the Multisport workout, and then click on the **Create Workout** button.
  ➤ If you have created a multisport workout before: Click on the More Options icon ⬤, and then click on the **Create Workout** button.
❖ Click on the **Add** button, and then click an activity.
❖ Keep adding activities by clicking on the Add button for each activity.
❖ Click on Untitled under Custom Tile, and then give the workout a name.

❖ After adding all the activities, click on the **Create Workout** button to store the workout.
❖ When you are ready to start a multisport workout, launch the Workout application, scroll to the Multisport workout, click on the More Options icon ⚫, and then click on one of the workouts.

To remove a Multisport workout from your smartwatch, touch the More Options icon ⚫ on the Multisport workouts tile, click on the Edit button ⊘ beside the workout you plan on deleting, scroll down, click on the **Delete Workout** button, and then touch the **Delete** button.

Start a swimming workout

❖ Launch the Workout application.
❖ Roll the Digital Crown to Pool Swim or Open Water Swim.
For Pool Swim, set the length of the pool, and then click on **Start**

❖ When you are done, hold down the Digital Crown to unlock your smartwatch, click on the **End** button, and then click on the **End Workout** button.

To pause or resume your swimming workout, press the side button & Digital Crown simultaneously.

Manually clear water from your smartwatch after swimming

When you begin a swim workout, your watch will lock the screen with **Water Lock** to prevent accidental taps. When you are out of the water, hold down the Digital Crown to unlock your display and clear water from your smartwatch's speaker

❖ After swimming, press your watch's side button to reveal the Control Centre, and then click on the Water Lock button .
❖ Hold down the Digital Crown to unlock your display and clear water from your smartwatch's speaker.

Update your weight & height

❖ Launch the Watch application on your phone.
❖ Click on the **My Watch** tab, head over to Health> Health Detail, and then touch **Edit**.
❖ Click on Weight or Height, and then make the adjustments.

Change the measurement unit

You can change the measurement unit the Workout application uses.

❖ Navigate to the Settings application.
❖ Touch the **Workout** button, scroll, touch Unit of Measure, and then make the adjustments.

Automatically pause cycling & running workouts

❖ Launch the Settings application.
❖ Touch the **Workout** button, click on the **Auto-Pause** button, and then enable the **Auto-Pause** feature.

Your smartwatch will automatically pause & resume cycling & running workouts—for example, if you stop to drink water or cross the road.

Activate or deactivate workout reminders

For swimming, running, walking, & other exercises, your watch detects when you are moving and prompts you to start the Workout application. It'll still remind you to end the exercise when you stop. Adhere to the guidelines below to enable or deactivate workout reminders.

❖ Launch the Settings application.
❖ Touch the **Workout** button, and then change the End Workout Reminders & Start Workout Reminders setting.

Or, launch the Watch application on your phone, click on the **My Watch** button, click on the **Workout** button, and then make changes to the workout reminder settings.

Save power while working out

You can extend the battery life of your smartwatch while exercising.

❖ Launch the Settings application.
❖ Touch the **Workout** button, and then enable **Low Power Mode**.

INDEX

T

Theater, 6, 67, 68, 185

V

Voice Memos, 259, 260

W

watch face, 7, 12, 16, 27, 36, 51, 52, 61, 75, 84, 85, 86, 88, 117, 118, 120, 139, 161, 163, 165, 166, 167, 168, 169, 170, 171, 172, 190, 248
Water Lock, 288
Waypoint, 14, 21, 199, 200, 201
waypoints, 194

wheelchair, 18, 176, 277
Workout, 22, 53, 167, 175, 252, 274, 275, 276, 277, 278, 279, 280, 281, 282, 284, 285, 286, 287, 288, 289, 290, 291
wrist, 5, 14, 18, 11, 29, 36, 37, 40, 41, 44, 45, 61, 80, 82, 102, 104, 107, 148, 149, 150, 154, 183, 184, 185, 204, 207, 209, 217, 256, 267, 268, 272

Z

Zoom, 9, 124, 125, 126

Made in the USA
Middletown, DE
30 August 2024

60001043R00176